FABULOUS
COOKIES

FABULOUS
COOKIES

SCRUMPTIOUS RECIPES FOR
DELICIOUS HOMEMADE TREATS

Hilaire Walden

TED SMART

This edition produced for
The Book People Ltd
Hall Wood Avenue
Haydock
St Helens WA11 9UL

© 2001 Anness Publishing Limited
Hermes House, 88-89 Blackfriars Road, London SE1 8HA

Publisher: Joanna Lorenz
Project Editor: Joanne Rippin
Designer: Siân Keogh, Axis Design
Illustrator: Christos Chrysanthou, Axis Design
Cover Artwork: Balley Design Associates
Front cover: William Lingwood, Photographer; Helen Trent, Stylist; Sunil Vijayakar, Home Economist

1 3 5 7 9 10 8 6 4 2

The recipes in this book were supplied by: Liz Trigg, Patricia Lousada, Carla Capalbo, Laura Washburn, Frances Cleary, Norma MacMillan, Christine France, Pamela Westland, Hilaire Walden, Elizabeth Wolf-Cohen, Janice Murfitt, Carole Handslip, Steven Wheeler, Katherine Richmond, Joanna Farrow, Judy Williams, Sue Maggs, Carole Clements, Jacqueline Clark, Sarah Maxwell, Sallie Morris, Lesley Mackley, Roz Denny, Sarah Gates, Norma Miller, Maxine Clark, Shirley Gill, Judy Jackson, Gilly Love, Janet Brinkworth, Ruby Le Bois, Elisabeth Lambert Ortiz, Sohelia Kimberley.
Photography by: Karl Adamson, Edward Allright, Steve Baxter, James Duncan, John Freeman, Michelle Garrett, Nelson Hargreaves, Amanda Heywood, David Jordan, Patrick McLeavey, Michael Michaels, Polly Wreford.

Note
Medium eggs should be used unless otherwise stated.

Recipe for Icing Glaze
15ml/1 tbsp lightly beaten egg white
15ml/1 tbsp lemon juice
75–115g/3–4oz/¾–1 cup confectioners' sugar

Mix the egg white and lemon juice in a bowl. Gradually beat
in the confectioners' sugar until the mixture is smooth and
has the consistency of thin cream. The icing should coat the
back of a spoon.

Contents

Introduction

Americans call them cookies and the British traditionally use the term biscuits, although now the word cookie has become quite common all over the world.

Whichever name is used, sweet cookies are delicious to nibble at any time of the day: with a cup of tea or coffee, or to serve with ice cream or other light dessert.

The American word "cookie" is of Dutch origin, from the word *koekje* meaning little cake. The origins of "biscuit" are to be found in the word itself: it comes from the French *bis cuit*, meaning twice cooked, and goes back to the days when bakers put slices of newly-baked bread back into the cooking oven, so that they dried out completely, becoming something like a rusk. This was really a method of preservation for it enabled the cookies to be kept for a long time; so long, in fact that they could be taken as a basic food item, known as "ship's biscuits", on long sea voyages.

For many years housewives continued with the practice of drying their biscuits a second time, and it was not until the beginning of the last century that the habit died out. Then both the quality and variety of biscuits improved dramatically.

A batch of homemade cookies will fill your kitchen with a wonderful aroma when they are ready to come out of the oven. There is a great difference between homemade cookies and the commercial ones sold in shops and supermarkets. Packaged, mass-produced cookies are more concerned with profit and long shelf-life. They are usually too sweet, contain additives and their character and flavour, let alone purity, cannot compare with a tasty cookie from your own store cupboard. Home baked cookies mean you can choose to use only the best ingredients.

There is almost no end to the range of cookies that can be made at home, using recipes that, over the years, have become great favourites the world over, with adults, teenagers and children alike.

This comprehensive collection of recipes suits every occasion and every taste, no matter if the fancy is for something rich and indulgent or traditionally wholesome, delightfully crisp or moist and chewy, satisfyingly chunky or elegantly thin, nutty or chocolatey. This book will inspire you to bake your favourite cookies for high days, holidays and special occasions, keep some dough in the freezer for unexpected guests, and determine never again to resort to the supermarket for your cookies.

▶ *Cookies are not only ideal for everyday eating, or special treats at home; they can also be gift-wrapped and given away as a special gift.*

Cookie Tips
& Techniques

Store Cupboard

The ingredients for cookie making can be found in most people's store cupboards and fridges.

Chocolate Buy good quality chocolate with at least 50% cocoa solids for baking. Plain chocolate gives a distinctive strong, rich flavour while milk chocolate has a sweeter taste. White chocolate often does not contain any cocoa solids, and lacks the flavour of true chocolate. It is the most difficult chocolate to melt and has poor setting qualities.

Eggs Eggs should be at room temperature so, if you keep them in the fridge, move the number you want to room temperature at least 30 minutes before making a recipe.

Flours Flour provides the structure that makes the cookies. Always sift flour. Not only will this remove any lumps, which are rare nowadays, but lightens the flour by incorporating air, and makes it easier to mix in.

Self-raising flour has raising agents added and is the type of flour most usually used in straightforward cookies that need to rise.

Plain flour is used when rising is considered a fault, as when making shortbread. Rich or heavy mixtures that should be raised also often call for plain flour plus additional raising agents in the specific proportions required for the particular recipe.

Wholemeal flour adds more flavour than white flour and is the healthier option but does produce denser cookies. When lightness is important extra raising agents should be added. Some recipes work well with a mixture of white and wholemeal flour.

Dried fruits Today, most dried fruits are dried by artificial heat rather than by the sun, and are treated with sulphur dioxide to help their preservation. Oils are sometimes sprayed on to the fruit to give it a shiny appearance and to prevent them sticking together. Try to buy fruit which have been coated with vegetable oils not mineral oils.

Butter and margarine Butter gives the best flavour to cookies and should be used whenever possible, especially when there is a high fat content, as in shortbread. However, it can be used interchangeably with hard block margarine. Butter or margarine to be used for creaming with sugar needs to be at room temperature and softened. For rubbing in, the fat should be at a cool room temperature, not fridge hard, and chopped quite finely.

Soft margarine is really only suitable for making cookies by the all-in-one method and when the fat has to be melted.

Glacé fruits Wash glacé fruits before using them to remove the syrupy coating, then dry thoroughly.

Spices Ground cinnamon, ginger, mixed spice, nutmeg and cloves may be used in cookies. All spices should be as fresh as possible. Buy in small quantities to use within a few months.

Honey Honey adds its own distinctive flavour to cookies. It contains 17% water so you will need to use slightly more honey than sugar, and reduce the amounts of the other liquids used. For easy mixing in, use clear honey.

Sugars Caster sugar is the best sweetener to use for the creaming method because the crystals dissolve easily and quickly when creamed with the fat. Granulated sugar is coarser textured than caster sugar so this is best used for rubbed-in mixtures and when the sugar is heated with the fat or liquid until it dissolves. Icing sugar appears in the ingredients for some cookie recipes where it is important that the sugar dissolves very readily. Demerara sugar can be used when the sugar is dissolved over heat before being added to the dry ingredients. Soft light and dark brown sugars are used when a richer flavour and colour are called for.

Nuts Nuts become rancid if stored for too long, in the light or at too high a temperature, so only buy in amounts that you will use within 1-2 months and keep them in an airtight container in a cool, dark cupboard. Alternatively, freeze them for up to 1 year.

Equipment

A delightful aspect of cookie making is that it requires the minimum of special equipment.

You can make quite a range of cookies with just a mixing bowl, measures or weights, a wooden spoon, a baking sheet and a wire rack. Only a few items are needed to extend the range much further. Many supermarkets now sell all you will need for cookie making.

Baking tins Used good quality sturdy tins; thin, cheap tins will buckle with time. Cheap tins also heat more quickly so cookies are liable to cook quickly, brown and stick to them more readily. Non-stick tins, of course, save greasing, and lining when called for, greatly reduce sticking and cut down on washing up.

Cannelle knife This tool is great for carving stripes in the skin of citrus fruit. Pare off thin strips before slicing the fruit to make an attractive edge.

Cutters Cutters are available in many different shapes and sizes, ranging from simple plain biscuit circles in various sizes, to small cutters for *petits fours* and savoury cocktail nibbles, to animal shapes, hearts and flowers. For best results, the important criterion that applies to all cutters is that they should be sharp, to give a good clear, sharp outline. This really means that they should be made from metal; plastic cutters tend to compress the cut edges.

To use a cutter, press down firmly on the cutter so that it cuts straight down right through the dough. Then lift up the cutter, without twisting it.

If you want to cut out a shape for which you do not have a cutter, the thing to do is to make a template, or pattern. This is very easy.

Trace or draw the design on to greaseproof paper or card and cut it out using scissors. Lay the template on to the rolled out cookie dough. Use the point of a large, sharp knife to carefully cut around the template, taking care not to drag it. With a thin metal pallette knife or fish slice, transfer the shape to the prepared baking sheet, without distorting the shape.

Food processor Although food processors save time, their drawback is their very speed; they work so fast that you must be careful not to overmix a mixture. Food processors combine rather than beat ingredients together, so they are not so useful for recipes where lightness is important. Also, many models cannot whisk egg whites, and even in those designed for whisking, the whites will not become really stiff.

Knives A round-bladed knife can be used for the initial stages of cutting in the fat before it is rubbed in. Large, sharp knives are needed for cutting cleanly and efficiently through rolled-out dough, or refrigerated dough. Palette knives are invaluable for spreading and smoothing mixtures in cake tins, transferring cut out cookies to baking sheets before baking and then transferring the baked cookies to a wire rack to cool. They can also be used for spreading icing on cookies.

Measures A set of accurate measuring spoons is vital for measuring 15ml/1 tablespoon, 5ml/1 teaspoon and fractions of teaspoons. All the amounts given in recipes are for level spoonfuls unless otherwise stated. For liquids, use a heatproof jug, preferably see-through, that is calibrated for both imperial and metric measures.

Pastry brushes A large pastry brush is very useful for brushing surplus flour from work surfaces and cookie doughs that are being rolled out, and for greasing cake tins. A pastry brush is also needed for brushing on glazes. Buy good quality brushes with firmly-fixed bristles.

Piping bags and nozzles A medium piping bag with a selection of nozzles is very useful to have for piping uncooked cookie dough, and for decorating cookies after baking. Use small disposable piping bags for chocolate or icing, where a fine line is required.

Rolling pin Rolling pins made of wood are the most common, but you can now buy marble or even plastic ones which are considered to be more hygienic.

Scales A good set of scales is essential for successful cookie making. Whether you use spring balance, modern electronic or old-fashioned balanced scales with a set of weights, test them frequently for accuracy by putting something on them which has the weight printed on it.

Sieves If possible have a set of strong sieves in 2 or 3 different sizes.

Skewers and cocktail sticks Either of these can be used for testing whether cookie mixtures are cooked.

Spatulas A flexible rubber spatula is indispensable for scraping every last morsel from the mixing bowl into the cake tin.

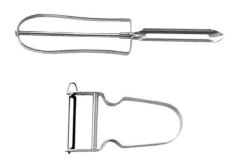

Swivel-blade peelers Both long-handled and broad-handled peelers are the best tools for peeling fruit.

Tea strainer A tea strainer will come in handy for sifting icing sugar over cookies as last-minute decoration.

Whisk Use either a wire balloon whisk or a rotary whisk for beating eggs together. It is a good idea to have two sizes of balloon whisks, to suit the amount of mixture.

Zester Ideal for citrus fruit, a zester has the same function as a cannelle knife but produces a row of thin stripes.

Measuring ingredients

Cooks with years of experience may not need to measure ingredients, but if you are a beginner or are trying a new recipe for the first time, it is best to follow instructions carefully. Also, measuring ingredients precisely will ensure consistent results.

1 For liquids measured in pints or litres: use a glass or clear plastic measuring jug. Put it on a flat surface and pour in the liquid. Bend down and check that the liquid is level with the marking on the jug, as specified in the recipe.

2 For liquids measured in spoons: pour the liquid into the measuring spoon, to the brim, and then pour it into the mixing bowl. Do not hold the spoon over the bowl when measuring because some liquid may overflow.

3 For measuring dry ingredients in a spoon: fill the spoon, scooping up the ingredient. Level the surface with the rim of the spoon, using the straight edge of a knife.

4 For measuring dry ingredients by weight: scoop or pour on to the scales, watching the dial or reading carefully. Balance scales give more accurate readings than spring scales.

5 For measuring syrups: set the mixing bowl on the scales and turn the gauge to zero, or make a note of the weight. Pour in the required weight of syrup.

6 For measuring butter: cut with a sharp knife and weigh, or cut off the specified amount following the markings on the wrapping paper.

Making cookies by the rubbing in method

Plain cookies are usually made by rubbing the fat into the flour. For this, the fat, whether butter, margarine or lard, should be neither rock hard from the fridge, nor too warm. It is first chopped into small pieces, then added to the dry ingredients in a bowl. The mixture is lifted high and the lumps of fat rubbed between the fingertips as the mixture is allowed to fall back into the bowl.

1 Sift the flour into a bowl, adding the raising agents, salt and any sugar or spices and mix them evenly.

2 Stir in any other dry ingredients; combine the oats or other cereal, or coconut. Add the butter or margarine, cut into pieces.

3 Sprinkle the liquid ingredients (water, cream, milk, buttermilk or beaten egg) over the mixture.

4 Mix with your fingers or stir with a fork until the dry ingredients are thoroughly moistened and will come together in a ball of fairly soft dough in the centre of the bowl.

5 Press the dough into a ball. If it is too dry to form a dough, add some extra water.

6 Turn the dough on to a lightly floured surface. Knead very lightly, folding and pressing, to mix evenly – about 30 seconds. Wrap the ball of dough in clear film or greaseproof paper and chill it for at least 30 minutes.

Making cookies by the creaming method

To make cookies by the creaming method, the fat and sugar are 'creamed' – or beaten – together before the eggs and dry ingredients are added. The fat (usually butter or margarine) should be soft enough to be beaten so, if necessary, remove it from the refrigerator and leave for at least 30 minutes. For best results, the eggs should be at room temperature.

1 Sift the flour with the salt, raising agent(s) and any other dry ingredients, such as spices or cocoa powder, into a bowl. Set aside.

2 Put the fat in a large, deep bowl and beat with an electric mixer at medium speed, or a wooden spoon, until the texture is soft and pliable.

3 Add the sugar to the creamed fat gradually. With the mixer at medium-high speed, or using the wooden spoon, beat it into the fat until the mixture is pale and very fluffy. The sugar should be completely incorporated.

5 Add the dry ingredients to the mixture. Beat at low speed just until smoothly combined, or fold in with a large metal spoon.

6 If the recipe calls for any liquid, add it in small portions alternately with portions of the dry ingredients.

7 If the recipe specifies, whisk egg whites separately until frothy, add sugar and continue whisking until stiff peaks form. Fold into the mixture.

Making cookies by the all-in-one method

Some cookies are made by an easy all-in-one method where all the ingredients are combined in a bowl and beaten thoroughly. The mixture can also be made in a food processor, but take care not to over-process. A refinement on the all-in-one method is to separate the eggs and make the mixture with the yolks. The whites are whisked separately and then folded in. Soft margarine has to be used.

4 Add the eggs or egg yolks, one at a time, beating well after each addition. Scrape the bowl often so all the ingredients are evenly combined. If the mixture curdles, add 15ml/1 tbsp of the measured flour.

8 Pour the mixture into a prepared cake tin and bake as specified.

1 Sift the flour and any other dry ingredients such as salt, raising agents and spices, into a bowl.

2 Add the liquid ingredients, such as eggs, melted or soft fat, milk or fruit juices, and beat until smooth, with an electric mixer for speed. Pour into the prepared tins and bake as specified in the recipe.

Traditional Cookies

Granola Cookies

Makes 18

INGREDIENTS

*115g/4oz/¹/₂ cup butter or
margarine
75g/3oz/¹/₂ cup light brown sugar
75g/3oz/¹/₃ cup crunchy
peanut butter
1 egg
50g/2oz/¹/₂ cup plain flour
2.5ml/¹/₂ tsp baking powder
2.5ml/¹/₂ tsp ground cinnamon
pinch of salt
225g/8oz/2 cups muesli
50g/2oz/¹/₃ cup raisins
50g/2oz/¹/₂ cup walnuts, chopped*

1 Preheat the oven to 180°C/350°F/ Gas 4. Grease a baking sheet. Put the butter or margarine in a bowl.

2 With an electric mixer, cream the butter or margarine and sugar until light and fluffy. Beat in the peanut butter, then beat in the egg.

3 Sift the flour, baking powder, cinnamon and salt over the peanut butter mixture and stir to blend. Stir in the muesli, raisins, and walnuts. Taste the mixture to see if it needs more sugar, as mueslis vary in sweetness.

4 Drop rounded tablespoonfuls of the batter on to the prepared baking sheet about 2.5cm/1in apart. Press gently with the back of a spoon to spread each mound into a circle.

5 Bake for about 15 minutes until lightly coloured. With a metal spatula, transfer to a wire rack and leave to cool.

Crunchy Oatmeal Cookies

Makes 14

INGREDIENTS

*175g/6oz/³/₄ cup butter or
margarine
125g/4¹/₂oz/³/₄ cup caster sugar
1 egg yolk
175g/6oz/1¹/₂ cups plain flour
5ml/1 tsp bicarbonate of soda
pinch of salt
40g/1¹/₂oz/¹/₂ cup rolled oats
40g/1¹/₂oz/¹/₂ cup crunchy
nugget cereal*

Variation For Nutty Oatmeal Cookies, substitute an equal quantity of chopped walnuts or pecans for the cereal, and prepare as described.

1 With an electric mixer, cream the butter or margarine and sugar together until light and fluffy. Mix in the egg yolk.

2 Sift over the flour, bicarbonate of soda and salt, then stir into the butter mixture. Add the oats and cereal and stir to blend. Chill for at least 20 minutes.

3 Preheat the oven to 190°C/375°F/ Gas 5. Grease a baking sheet. Flour the bottom of a glass.

4 Roll the dough into balls. Place them on the prepared baking sheet and flatten with the bottom of the glass.

5 Bake for 10–12 minutes until golden. With a metal spatula, transfer to a wire rack to cool completely.

Coconut Oat Cookies

Makes 18

❦

INGREDIENTS

175g/6oz/2 cups quick-cooking oats
75g/3oz/1 cup shredded coconut.
225g/8oz/1 cup butter or margarine, at room temperature
115g/4oz/½ cup granulated sugar
40g/1½oz/¼ cup firmly packed dark brown sugar
2 eggs
60ml/4 tbsp milk
7.5ml/1½ tsp vanilla essence
115g/4oz/1 cup plain flour
2.5ml/½ tsp bicarbonate of soda
pinch of salt
5ml/1 tsp ground cinnamon

❦

1 Preheat the oven to 200°C/400°F/Gas 6. Lightly grease two baking sheets. Grease the bottom of a glass and dip in sugar.

2 Spread the oats and coconut on an ungreased baking sheet. Bake for 8–10 minutes until golden brown, stirring occasionally.

3 With an electric mixer, cream the butter or margarine and both sugars until light and fluffy. Beat in the eggs, one at a time, then add the milk and vanilla essence. Sift over the dry ingredients and fold in. Stir in the oats and coconut.

4 Drop spoonfuls of the dough 2.5–5cm/1–2in apart on the baking sheets and flatten with the glass. Bake for 8–10 minutes. Transfer to a wire rack to cool.

Crunchy Jumbles

Makes 36

❦

INGREDIENTS

115g/4oz/½ cup butter or margarine, at room temperature
225g/8oz/1 cup sugar
1 egg
5ml/1 tsp vanilla essence
175g/6oz/1¼ cups plain flour
2.5ml/½ tsp bicarbonate of soda
pinch of salt
115g/4oz/2 cups crisped rice cereal
1 cup chocolate chips

❦

Variation For even crunchier cookies, add ½ cup walnuts, coarsely chopped, with the cereal and chocolate chips.

1 Preheat the oven to 180°C/350°F/Gas 4. Lightly grease two baking sheets.

2 With an electric mixer, cream the butter or margarine and sugar until light and fluffy. Beat in the egg and vanilla. Sift over the flour, bicarbonate of soda, and salt and fold in.

3 Add the cereal and chocolate chips. Stir to mix thoroughly.

4 Drop spoonfuls of the dough 2.5–5cm/1–2in apart on the prepared sheets. Bake for 10–12 minutes until golden. Transfer to a wire rack to cool.

Malted Oaty Crisps

These cookies are very crisp and crunchy – ideal to serve with morning coffee.

Makes 18

❦

INGREDIENTS

175g/6oz/1¹/₂ cups rolled oats
75g/3oz/¹/₄ cup light
muscovado sugar
1 egg
60ml/4 tbsp sunflower oil
30ml/2 tbsp malt extract

❦

1 Preheat the oven to 190°C/375°F/
Gas 5. Lightly grease two baking
sheets. Mix the rolled oats and brown
sugar in a bowl, breaking up any
lumps in the sugar. Add the egg,
sunflower oil and malt extract, mix
well, then leave to soak for 15 minutes.

2 Using a teaspoon, place small
heaps of the mixture well apart
on the prepared baking sheets. Press
the heaps into 7.5cm/3in rounds with
the back of a dampened fork.

3 Bake for 10–15 minutes, until
golden brown. Leave to cool for
1 minute, then remove with a palette
knife and cool on a wire rack.

Variation To give these crisp biscuits a
coarser texture, substitute jumbo oats
for some or all of the rolled oats.

Shortbread

Makes 8

🌿

INGREDIENTS

*175g/6oz/²/₃ cup unsalted butter
115g/4oz/¹/₂ cup caster sugar
150g/5oz/1¹/₄ cups plain flour
50g/2oz/¹/₂ cup rice flour
1.5ml/¹/₄ tsp baking powder
pinch of salt*

🌿

1 Preheat the oven to 160°C/325°F/
Gas 3. Grease a shallow 20cm/8in
cake tin.

2 With an electric mixer, cream the
butter and sugar together until
light and fluffy. Sift over the flours,
baking powder and salt and mix well.

3 Press the dough neatly into the
prepared tin, smoothing the
surface with the back of a spoon.
Prick all over with a fork, then score
into eight equal wedges.

4 Bake for 40–45 minutes. Leave in
the tin until cool enough to
handle, then unmould and recut the
wedges while still hot.

Oatmeal Wedges

Makes 8

🌿

INGREDIENTS

*50g/2oz/4 tbsp butter
25ml/1¹/₂ tbsp treacle
50g/2oz/¹/₃ cup dark brown sugar
175g/6oz/1¹/₄ cups rolled oats
pinch of salt*

🌿

Variation If wished, add 5ml/1 tsp
ground ginger to the melted butter.

1 Preheat the oven to 180°C/350°F/
Gas 4. Line a 20cm/8in shallow
cake tin with greaseproof paper and
grease the paper.

2 Place the butter, treacle and sugar
in a saucepan over a low heat.
Cook, stirring, until melted and
combined.

3 Remove from the heat and add
the oats and salt. Stir to blend.

4 Spoon into the prepared cake tin
and smooth the surface. Bake for
20–25 minutes until golden brown.
Leave in the tin until cool enough to
handle, then unmould and cut into
eight equal wedges while still hot.

Melting Moments

These cookies are very crisp and light – and they melt in your mouth.

Makes 16–20

INGREDIENTS

40g/1¹/₂oz/3 tbsp butter or margarine
65g/2¹/₂oz/5 tbsp lard
75g/3oz/¹/₂ cup caster sugar
¹/₂ egg, beaten
few drops of vanilla or almond essence
150g/5oz/1¹/₄ cups self-raising flour
rolled oats for coating
4–5 glacé cherries, quartered

1 Preheat the oven to 180°C/350°F/ Gas 4. Grease two baking sheets. Cream together the butter or margarine, lard and sugar, then gradually beat in the egg and vanilla or almond essence.

2 Stir the flour into the beaten mixture, then roll into 16–20 small balls in your hands.

3 Spread the rolled oats on a sheet of greaseproof paper and toss the balls in them to coat evenly.

4 Place the balls, spaced slightly apart, on the prepared baking sheets, place a piece of cherry on top of each and bake for 15–20 minutes, until lightly browned. Allow the cookies to cool for a few minutes before transferring to a wire rack.

Chocolate Chip Hazelnut Cookies

Chocolate chip cookies, with a delicious nutty flavour.

Makes 36

INGREDIENTS

115g/4oz/1 cup plain flour
5ml/1 tsp baking powder
pinch of salt
75g/3oz/⅓ cup butter or
margarine
115g/4oz/1½ cups caster sugar
50g/2oz/⅓ cup light brown sugar
1 egg
5ml/1 tsp vanilla essence
125g/4½oz/⅔ cup chocolate chips
50g/2oz/½ cup hazelnuts,
chopped

1 Preheat the oven to 180°C/350°F/ Gas 4. Grease 2–3 baking sheets. Sift the flour, baking powder and salt into a small bowl. Set aside.

2 With an electric mixer, cream together the butter or margarine and the sugars. Beat in the egg and vanilla essence. Add the flour mixture and beat well with the mixer on low speed.

3 Stir in the chocolate chips and half of the hazelnuts, using a wooden spoon.

4 Drop teaspoonfuls of the mixture on to the prepared baking sheets, to form 2cm/¾in mounds. Space the cookies 2.5–5cm/1–2in apart.

5 Flatten each cookie lightly with a wet fork. Sprinkle the remaining hazelnuts on top of the cookies and press lightly into the surface.

6 Bake for 10–12 minutes until golden. Transfer the biscuits to a wire rack and leave to cool.

Chocolate Chip Oat Biscuits

Makes 60

❦

INGREDIENTS

115g/4oz/1 cup plain flour
2.5ml/¹/₂ tsp bicarbonate of soda
1.5ml/¹/₄ tsp baking powder
pinch of salt
115g/4oz/¹/₂ cup butter or margarine
115g/4oz/¹/₂ cup caster sugar
90g/3¹/₂oz/generous ¹/₂ cup light brown sugar
1 egg
¹/₂ tsp vanilla essence
75g/3oz/³/₄ cup rolled oats
175g/6oz/1 cup plain chocolate chips

❦

1 Preheat the oven to 180°C/350°F/ Gas 4. Grease 3–4 baking sheets.

2 Sift the flour, bicarbonate of soda, baking powder and salt into a mixing bowl. Set aside.

3 With an electric mixer, cream together the butter or margarine and the sugars. Add the egg and vanilla essence and beat until light and fluffy.

4 Add the flour mixture and beat on a low speed until thoroughly blended. Stir in the rolled oats and chocolate chips. The dough should be crumbly. Drop heaped teaspoonfuls on to the prepared baking sheets, spacing the dough about 2.5cm/1in apart.

5 Bake for about 15 minutes until just firm around the edge but still soft to the touch in the centre. With a slotted spatula, transfer the biscuits to a wire rack and leave to cool.

Mexican Almond Cookies

Light and crisp, these biscuits are perfect with a cup of strong coffee.

Makes 24

INGREDIENTS

115g/4oz/1 cup plain flour
175g/6oz/1⅓ cups icing sugar
pinch of salt
50g/2oz/½ cup almonds, finely chopped
2.5ml/½ tsp vanilla essence
115g/4oz/½ cup unsalted butter
icing sugar for dusting

Variation Try using other nuts such as walnuts, peanuts or pecans.

1 Preheat the oven to 180°C/350°F/ Gas 4. Sift the flour, icing sugar and salt into a bowl. Add the almonds and mix well. Stir in the vanilla essence.

2 Using your fingertips, work the butter into the mixture to make a dough. Form it into a ball.

3 Roll out the dough on a lightly floured surface until it is 3mm/⅛in thick. Using a round cutter, stamp out into about 24 biscuits, re-rolling the trimmings as necessary.

4 Transfer the biscuits to non-stick baking sheets and bake for 30 minutes, until browned. Transfer to wire racks to cool, then dust thickly with icing sugar.

Peanut Butter Cookies

For extra crunch add 50g/2oz/¹/₂ cup chopped peanuts with the peanut butter.

Makes 24

❧

INGREDIENTS

*115g/4oz/1 cup plain flour
2.5ml/¹/₂ tsp bicarbonate of soda
pinch of salt
115g/4oz/¹/₂ cup butter
125g/4¹/₂oz/³/₄ cup firmly packed
light brown sugar
1 egg
5ml/1 tsp vanilla essence
225g/8oz/1 cup crunchy peanut
butter*

❧

1 Sift together the flour, bicarbonate of soda and salt and set aside.

2 With an electric mixer, cream together the butter and sugar until light and fluffy.

3 In another bowl, mix the egg and vanilla essence, then gradually beat into the butter mixture.

4 Stir in the peanut butter and blend thoroughly. Stir in the dry ingredients. Chill for at least 30 minutes, until firm.

5 Preheat the oven to 180°C/350°F/ Gas 4. Grease two baking sheets.

6 Spoon out rounded teaspoonfuls of the dough and roll into balls.

7 Place the balls on the prepared baking sheets and press flat with a fork into circles about 6cm/2¹/₂in in diameter, making a criss-cross pattern. Bake for 12–15 minutes, until lightly coloured. Transfer to a wire rack to cool.

Tollhouse Cookies

Makes 24

INGREDIENTS

*115g/4oz/¹/₂ cup butter or
margarine
50g/2oz/¹/₄ cup granulated sugar
75g/3oz/¹/₂ cup dark brown sugar
1 egg
2.5ml/¹/₂ tsp vanilla essence
125g/4¹/₂oz/1¹/₈ cups flour
2.5ml/¹/₂ tsp bicarbonate of soda
pinch of salt
175g/6oz/1 cup chocolate chips
50g/2oz/¹/₂ cup walnuts, chopped*

1 Preheat the oven to 180°C/350°F/ Gas 4. Grease two baking sheets.

2 With an electric mixer, cream together the butter or margarine and the two sugars until the mixture is light and fluffy.

3 In another bowl, mix the egg and vanilla essence, then gradually beat into the butter mixture. Sift over the flour, bicarbonate of soda and salt. Stir to blend.

4 Add the chocolate chips and walnuts, and mix to combine thoroughly.

5 Place heaped teaspoonfuls of the dough 5cm/2in apart on the prepared baking sheets. Bake for 10–15 minutes until lightly coloured. With a metal spatula, transfer to a wire rack to cool.

Snickerdoodles

Makes 30

❦

INGREDIENTS

115g/4oz/½ cup butter
115g/4oz/1½ cups caster sugar
5ml/1 tsp vanilla essence
2 eggs
50ml/2fl oz/¼ cup milk
400g/14oz/3½ cups plain flour
1 tsp bicarbonate of soda
50g/2oz/½ cup walnuts or pecans,
finely chopped
For the coating
75ml/5 tbsp sugar
30ml/2 tbsp ground cinnamon

❦

1 With an electric mixer, beat the butter until light and creamy. Add the sugar and vanilla essence and continue until fluffy. Beat in the eggs, then the milk.

2 Sift the flour and bicarbonate of soda over the butter mixture and stir to blend. Stir in the nuts. Refrigerate for 15 minutes. Preheat the oven to 190°C/375°F/Gas 5. Grease two baking sheets.

3 To make the coating, mix the sugar and cinnamon. Roll tablespoonfuls of the dough into walnut-size balls. Roll the balls in the sugar mixture. You may need to work in batches.

4 Place the balls 5cm/2in apart on the prepared baking sheets and flatten slightly. Bake for about 10 minutes until golden. Transfer to a wire rack to cool.

Chewy Chocolate Cookies

Makes 18

❦

INGREDIENTS

4 egg whites
300g/11oz/2½ cups icing sugar
115g/4oz/1 cup cocoa powder
30ml/2 tbsp plain flour
5ml/1 tsp instant coffee powder
15ml/1 tbsp water
115g/4oz/1 cup walnuts, finely
chopped

❦

1 Preheat the oven to 180°C/350°F/ Gas 4. Line two baking sheets with greaseproof paper and then grease the paper well.

2 With an electric mixer, beat the egg whites until frothy.

3 Sift the sugar, cocoa, flour and coffee into the whites. Add the water and continue beating on low speed to blend, then on high for a few minutes until the mixture thickens. With a rubber spatula, fold in the walnuts.

4 Place generous spoonfuls of the mixture 2.5cm/1in apart on the prepared baking sheets. Bake for 12–15 minutes until firm and cracked on top but soft on the inside. With a metal spatula, transfer to a wire rack to cool.

Variation Add 75g/3oz/½ cup chocolate chips to the dough with the chopped walnuts.

Buttermilk Cookies

Makes 15

INGREDIENTS

175g/6oz/1½ cups plain flour
pinch of salt
5ml/1 tsp baking powder
2.5ml/½ tsp bicarbonate of soda
50g/2oz/4 tbsp cold butter or margarine
175ml/6fl oz/¾ cup buttermilk

1 Preheat the oven to 220°C/425°F/ Gas 7. Grease a baking sheet.

2 Sift the dry ingredients into a bowl. Rub in the butter or margarine until the mixture resembles coarse crumbs.

3 Gradually pour in the buttermilk, stirring with a fork until the mixture forms a soft dough.

4 Roll out to about 1cm/½in thick. Stamp out 15 5cm/2in circles with a biscuit cutter.

5 Place on the prepared baking sheet and bake for 12–15 minutes until golden. Serve warm or at room temperature.

Baking Powder Cookies

These make a simple accompaniment to meals, or a snack with fruit preserves.

Makes 8

INGREDIENTS

165g/5½oz/1⅓ cups plain flour
30ml/2 tbsp sugar
15ml/1 tbsp baking powder
pinch of salt
40g/1½oz/5 tbsp cold butter, chopped
120ml/4fl oz/½ cup milk

Variation For Berry Shortcake, split the cookies in half while still warm. Butter one half, top with lightly sugared fresh berries, such as strawberries, raspberries or blueberries, and sandwich with the other half. Serve with dollops of whipped cream.

1 Preheat the oven to 220°C/425°F/ Gas 7. Grease a baking sheet. Sift the flour, sugar, baking powder and salt into a bowl.

2 Rub in the butter until the mixture resembles coarse crumbs. Pour in the milk and stir with a fork to form a soft dough.

3 Roll out the dough to about 5mm/¼in thick. Stamp out circles with a 6cm/2½in biscuit cutter.

4 Place on the prepared baking sheet and bake for about 12 minutes, until golden. Serve these soft biscuits hot or warm, spread with butter for meals. To accompany tea or coffee, serve with butter and jam or honey.

Traditional Sugar Cookies

Makes 36

❧

INGREDIENTS

350g/12oz/3 cups plain flour
5ml/1 tsp bicarbonate of soda
10ml/2 tsp baking powder
2.5ml/¹/₂ tsp grated nutmeg
115g/4oz/¹/₂ cup butter or
margarine
225g/8oz/1 cup caster sugar
2.5ml/¹/₂ tsp vanilla essence
1 egg
115g/4oz/¹/₂ cup milk
coloured or demerara sugar for
sprinkling

❧

1 Sift the flour, bicarbonate of soda, baking powder and nutmeg into a small bowl. Set aside.

2 With an electric mixer, cream together the butter or margarine, caster sugar and vanilla essence until the mixture is light and fluffy. Add the egg and beat to mix well.

3 Add the flour mixture alternately with the milk to make a soft dough. Wrap in clear film and chill for at least 30 minutes.

4 Preheat the oven to 180°C/350°F/ Gas 4. Roll out the dough on a lightly floured surface to 3mm/¹/₈in thick. Cut into rounds or other shapes with floured biscuit cutters.

5 Transfer to ungreased baking sheets. Sprinkle with sugar. Bake for 10–12 minutes until golden brown. Transfer the cookies to a wire rack to cool.

Brittany Butter Cookies

These little biscuits are similar to shortbread, but richer. Traditionally, they are made with lightly salted butter.

Makes 18–20

❦

INGREDIENTS

6 egg yolks, lightly beaten
15ml/1 tbsp milk
250g/9 oz/2¼ cups plain flour
175g/6oz/¾ cup caster sugar
200g/7oz/scabt 1cup butter

❦

1 Preheat the oven to 180°C/350°F/ Gas 4. Butter a heavy baking sheet. Mix 15ml/1 tbsp of the egg yolks with the milk to make a glaze.

2 Sift the flour into a bowl. Add the egg yolks, sugar and butter and, work them together until creamy.

3 Gradually bring in a little flour at a time until it forms a slightly sticky dough.

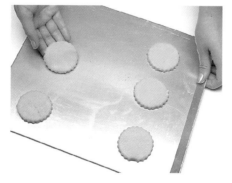

4 Using floured hands, pat out the dough to about 5mm/¼in thick and cut out rounds using a 7.5cm/3in cutter. Transfer the rounds to the prepared baking sheet, brush each with a little egg glaze, then, using the back of a knife, score with lines to create a lattice pattern.

5 Bake for about 12–15 minutes, until golden. Cool in the tin on a wire rack for 15 minutes, then carefully remove the biscuits and leave to cool completely on the rack.

Cook's Tip To make a large Brittany Butter Cake, pat the dough with well-floured hands into a 23cm/9in loose-based cake tin or springform tin. Brush with egg glaze and score the lattice pattern on top. Bake for 45 minutes– 1 hour, until firm to the touch and golden brown.

Toffee Cookies

Makes 36

❦

INGREDIENTS

175g/6oz/³/₄ cup unsalted butter, melted
200g/7oz/1³/₄ cups instant porridge oats
115g/4oz/packed ¹/₂ cup soft light brown sugar
120ml/4fl oz/¹/₂ cup corn syrup
30ml/2 tbsp vanilla essence
large pinch of salt
175g/6oz/³/₄ cup plain chocolate, grated
40g/1¹/₂oz/¹/₃ cup chopped walnuts

❦

1 Preheat the oven to 200°C/400°F/ Gas 6. Grease a 37.5 x 25cm/15 x 10in baking tin.

2 Mix together the butter, oats, sugar, syrup, vanilla essence and salt and press into the prepared tin. Bake for about 15–18 minutes, until the mixture is brown and bubbly.

3 Remove from the oven and immediately sprinkle on the chocolate. Set aside for 10 minutes, then spread the chocolate over the base. Sprinkle on the nuts. Transfer to a wire rack to cool. Cut into squares.

Rosewater Thins

These light, crunchy biscuits are easy to make and bake in minutes.

Makes 60

❦

INGREDIENTS

225g/8oz/1 cup slightly salted butter
225g/8oz/1 cup caster sugar
1 egg
15ml/1 tbsp single cream
300g/11oz/2¹/₂ cups plain flour
pinch of salt
5ml/1 tsp baking powder
15ml/1 tbsp rosewater
caster sugar for sprinkling

❦

1 Preheat the oven to 190°C/375°F/ Gas 5. Line two baking sheets with non-stick baking paper.

2 Soften the butter and mix with all the other ingredients until you have a firm dough. Mould the mixture into an even roll and wrap in greaseproof paper. Chill until it is firm enough to slice very thinly. This will take 1–1¹/₂ hours.

3 Arrange the cookies on the prepared baking sheets with enough space for them to spread. Sprinkle with a little caster sugar and bake for about 10 minutes until they are just turning brown at the edges.

Old-fashioned Ginger Cookies

Makes 60

INGREDIENTS

300g/11oz/2¹/₂ cups plain flour
5ml/1 tsp bicarbonate of soda
7.5ml/1¹/₂ tsp ground ginger
1.5ml/¹/₄ tsp ground cinnamon
1.5ml/¹/₄ tsp ground cloves
115g/4oz/¹/₂ cup butter or
margarine
350g/12oz/1¹/₂ cups caster sugar
1 egg, beaten
60ml/4 tbsp black treacle
5ml/1 tsp fresh lemon juice

1 Preheat the oven to 160°C/325°F/ Gas 3. Grease 3–4 baking trays.

2 Sift the flour, bicarbonate of soda and spices into a small bowl. Set aside.

3 With an electric mixer, cream together the butter or margarine and two-thirds of the sugar.

4 Stir in the egg, treacle and lemon juice. Add the flour mixture and mix in thoroughly with a wooden spoon to make a soft dough.

5 Shape the dough into 2cm/³/₄ in balls. Roll the balls in the remaining sugar and place them about 5cm/2in apart on the prepared baking trays.

6 Bake for about 12 minutes until the biscuits are just firm to the touch. With a slotted spatula, transfer the biscuits to a wire rack and leave to cool.

Chunky Chocolate Drops

Do not allow these cookies to cool completely on the baking sheet or they will become too crisp and will break when you try to lift them.

Makes 18

INGREDIENTS

175g/6oz plain chocolate, chopped
115g/4oz/½ cup unsalted butter, chopped
2 eggs
90g/3½oz/½ cup granulated sugar
50g/2oz/⅓ cup light brown sugar
40g/1½oz/⅓ cup plain flour
25g/1oz/¼ cup cocoa powder
5ml/1 tsp baking powder
10ml/2 tsp vanilla essence
pinch of salt
115g/4oz/1 cup pecans, toasted and coarsely chopped
175g/6oz/1 cup plain chocolate chips
115g/4oz fine quality white chocolate, chopped into 5mm/¼in pieces
115g/4oz fine quality milk chocolate, chopped into 5mm/¼in pieces

1 Preheat the oven to 160°C/325°F/ Gas 3. Grease two large baking sheets. In a medium saucepan over a low heat, melt the plain chocolate and butter, stirring until smooth. Remove from the heat and set aside to cool slightly.

2 In a large mixing bowl, using an electric mixer, beat the eggs and sugars for 2–3 minutes, until pale and creamy. Gradually pour in the melted chocolate mixture, beating until well blended. Beat in the flour, cocoa powder, baking powder, vanilla essence and salt until just blended. Stir in the nuts, chocolate chips and chocolate pieces.

3 Drop heaped tablespoons of the mixture on to the prepared baking sheets 10cm/4in apart. Flatten each to 7.5cm/3in rounds. Bake for 8–10 minutes, until the tops are shiny and cracked and the edges look crisp; do not over-bake or the cookies will become fragile.

4 Remove the baking sheets to a wire rack to cool for 2 minutes, then transfer to the rack to cool completely.

Orange Shortbread Fingers

These are a real tea-time treat. The fingers will keep in an airtight container for up to 2 weeks.

Makes 18

INGREDIENTS

115g/4oz/½ cup unsalted butter
50g/2oz/4 tbsp caster sugar, plus
extra for sprinkling
finely grated rind of 2 oranges
175g/6oz/1½ cups plain flour

1 Preheat the oven to 190°C/375°F/ Gas 5. Grease a large baking sheet. Beat together the butter and sugar until soft and creamy. Beat in the orange rind.

2 Gradually add the flour and gently pull the dough together to form a soft ball. Roll out the dough on a lightly floured surface to about 1cm/½in thick. Cut into fingers, sprinkle over a little extra caster sugar and put on the baking sheet. Prick the fingers with a fork and bake for about 20 minutes, until the fingers are a light golden colour.

Double Chocolate Cookies

Keep these luscious treats under lock and key unless you're feeling generous.

Makes 18–20

INGREDIENTS

115g/4oz/½ cup unsalted butter
115g/4oz/⅔ cup light muscovado
sugar
1 egg
5ml/1 tsp vanilla essence
150g/5oz/1¼ cups self-raising
flour
75g/3oz/¾ cup porridge oats
115g/4oz plain chocolate, roughly
chopped
115g/4oz white chocolate, roughly
chopped

Cook's Tip If you're short of time when making the cookies, substitute chocolate chips for the chopped chocolate. Chopped stem ginger would make a delicious addition as well.

1 Preheat the oven to 190°C/375°F/ Gas 5. Lightly grease two baking sheets. Cream the butter with the sugar in a bowl until pale and fluffy. Add the egg and vanilla essence and beat well.

2 Sift the flour over the mixture and fold in lightly with a metal spoon, then add the oats and chopped plain and white chocolate and stir until evenly mixed.

3 Place small spoonfuls of the mixture in 18–20 rocky heaps on the prepared baking sheets, leaving space for spreading.

4 Bake for 15–20 minutes, until beginning to turn pale golden. Cool for 2–3 minutes on the baking sheets, then transfer to wire racks to cool completely.

Chocolate and Nut Refrigerator Cookies

The dough must be chilled thoroughly before it can be sliced and baked.

Makes 50

INGREDIENTS

225g/8oz/2 cups plain flour
pinch of salt
50g/2oz plain chocolate, chopped
225g/8oz/1 cup unsalted butter
225g/8oz/1 cup caster sugar
2 eggs
5ml/1 tsp vanilla essence
115g/4oz/1 cup walnuts, finely
chopped

Variation For two-tone cookies, melt only 25g/1oz chocolate. Combine all the ingredients, except the chocolate, as above. Divide the dough in half. Add the chocolate to one half. Roll out the plain dough on to a flat sheet. Roll out the chocolate dough, place on top of the plain dough and roll up. Wrap, slice and bake as described.

1 In a small bowl, sift together the flour and salt. Set aside. Melt the chocolate in the top of a double boiler, or in a heatproof bowl set over a saucepan of hot water. Set aside.

2 With an electric mixer, cream the butter until soft. Add the sugar and continue beating until the mixture is light and fluffy.

3 Mix the eggs with the vanilla essence, then gradually stir into the butter mixture.

4 Stir in the chocolate, then the flour followed by the nuts.

5 Divide the dough into four parts, and roll each into 5cm/2in diameter logs. Wrap tightly in foil and chill or freeze until firm.

6 Preheat the oven to 190°C/375°F/ Gas 5. Grease two baking sheets. Cut the dough into 5mm/¼in slices. Place on the prepared sheets and bake for about 10 minutes. Transfer to wire rack to cool.

Double Gingerbread Cookies

Packed in little bags or into a gingerbread box, these pretty cookies would make a lovely gift.

They are easy to make, but will have everyone wondering how you did it!

Makes 25

❧

INGREDIENTS

For the golden gingerbread
mixture
175g/6oz plain flour
1.5ml/¼ tsp bicarbonate of soda
pinch of salt
5ml/1 tsp ground cinnamon
*65g/2½oz unsalted butter, cut
in pieces*
75g/3oz caster sugar
*30ml/2 tbsp maple or
golden syrup*
1 egg yolk, beaten
For the chocolate gingerbread
mixture
175g/6oz/1½ cups plain flour
pinch of salt
10ml/2 tsp ground mixed spice
2.5ml/½ tsp bicarbonate of soda
25g/1oz/4 tbsp cocoa powder
*75g/3oz/⅓ cup unsalted butter,
chopped*
*75g/3oz/⅓ cup light muscovado
sugar*
1 egg, beaten

❧

1 To make the golden gingerbread
mixture, sift together the flour,
bicarbonate of soda, salt and spices.
Rub the butter into the flour in a
large bowl, until the mixture resembles
fine breadcrumbs. Add the sugar, syrup
and egg yolk and mix to a firm dough.
Knead lightly. Wrap in clear film and
chill for 30 minutes before shaping.

2 To make the chocolate gingerbread
mixture, sift together the flour,
salt, spice, bicarbonate of soda and
cocoa powder. Knead the butter into
the flour in a large bowl. Add the
sugar and egg and mix to a firm
dough. Knead lightly. Wrap in clear
film and chill for 30 minutes.

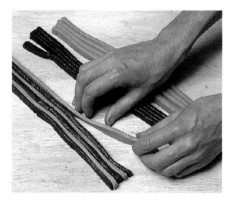

3 Roll out half of the chocolate
dough on a floured surface to a 28
x 4cm/11 x 1½in rectangle, 1cm/
½in thick. Repeat with half of the
golden gingerbread dough. Using a
knife, cut both lengths into seven long,
thin strips. Lay the strips together, side
by side, alternating the colours.

4 Roll out the remaining golden
gingerbread dough with your
hands to a long sausage, 2cm/¾in
wide and the length of the strips. Lay
the sausage of dough down the centre
of the striped dough.

5 Carefully bring the striped dough
up around the sausage and press
it gently in position, to enclose the
sausage completely. Roll the
remaining chocolate dough to a thin
rectangle measuring approximately
28 x 13cm/11 x 5in.

6 Bring the chocolate dough up
around the striped dough, to
enclose it. Press gently into place.
Wrap and chill for 30 minutes.

7 Preheat the oven to 180°C/350°F/
Gas 4. Grease a large baking
sheet. Cut the gingerbread roll into
thin slices and place them, slightly
apart, on the prepared baking sheet.

8 Bake for about 12–15 minutes,
until just beginning to colour
around the edges. Leave on the
baking sheet for 3 minutes and
transfer to a wire rack to cool
completely.

Spicy Pepper Biscuits

Makes 48

INGREDIENTS

200g/7oz/1¾ cups plain flour
50g/2oz/½ cup cornflour
10ml/2 tsp baking powder
2.5ml/½ tsp ground cardamom
2.5ml/½ tsp ground cinnamon
2.5ml/½ tsp grated nutmeg
2.5ml/½ tsp ground ginger
2.5ml/½ tsp ground allspice
pinch of salt
2.5ml/½ tsp freshly ground black
pepper
225g/8oz/1 cup butter or
margarine
90g/3½oz/1⅓ cups light brown
sugar
2.5ml/½ tsp vanilla essence
5ml/1 tsp finely grated lemon rind
50ml/2fl oz/¼ cup whipping
cream
75g/3oz/¾ cup finely ground
almonds
30ml/2 tbsp icing sugar

1 Preheat the oven to 180°C/350°F/ Gas 4.

2 Sift the flour, cornflour, baking powder, spices, salt and pepper into a bowl. Set aside.

3 With an electric mixer, cream the butter or margarine and brown sugar together until light and fluffy. Beat in the vanilla essence and grated lemon rind.

5 Shape the dough into 2cm/¾in balls. Place them on ungreased baking sheets, about 2.5cm/1in apart. Bake for 15–20 minutes until golden brown underneath.

4 With the mixer on low speed, add the flour mixture alternately with the whipping cream, beginning and ending with flour. Stir in the ground almonds.

6 Leave to cool on the baking sheets for about 1 minute before transferring to a wire rack to cool completely. Before serving, sprinkle lightly with icing sugar.

Aniseed Cookies

Makes 24

❦

INGREDIENTS

175g/6oz/1½ cups plain flour
5ml/1 tsp baking powder
pinch of salt
115g/4oz/½ cup unsalted butter
115g/4oz/½ cup caster sugar
1 egg
5ml/1 tsp whole aniseed
15ml/1 tbsp brandy
50g/2oz/¼ cup caster sugar mixed
with 2.5ml/½ tsp ground
cinnamon for sprinkling

❦

1 Sift together the flour, baking powder and salt. Set aside.

2 Beat the butter with the sugar until soft and fluffy. Add the egg, aniseed and brandy and beat until incorporated. Fold in the dry ingredients until just blended to a dough. Chill for 30 minutes.

3 Preheat the oven to 180°C/350°F/Gas 4. Grease two baking sheets.

4 On a lightly floured surface, roll out the chilled dough to about 3mm/⅛in thick.

5 With a floured cutter, pastry wheel or knife, cut out the biscuits into squares, diamonds or other shapes. The traditional shape for biscochitos is a fleur-de-lis but you might find this a bit too ambitious.

6 Place on the prepared baking sheets and sprinkle lightly with the cinnamon sugar.

7 Bake for about 10 minutes, until just barely golden. Cool on the baking sheet for 5 minutes before transferring to a wire rack to cool completely. The biscuits can be kept in an airtight container for up to one week.

Festive and Fancy Cookies

Lavender Heart Cookies

In folklore, lavender has always been linked with love, as has food, so make some heart-shaped cookies and serve them on Valentine's Day or any other romantic anniversary.

Makes 16–18

INGREDIENTS

115g/4oz/¹/₂ cup unsalted butter
50g/2oz/¹/₄ cup caster sugar
175g/6oz/1¹/₂ cups plain flour
30ml/2 tbsp fresh lavender florets
or 15ml/1 tbsp dried culinary
lavender, roughly chopped
30ml/2 tbsp superfine sugar for
sprinkling

1 Cream together the butter and sugar until fluffy. Stir in the flour and lavender and bring the mixture together in a soft ball. Cover and chill for 15 minutes.

2 Preheat the oven to 200°C/400°F/ Gas 6. Roll out the dough on a lightly floured surface and stamp out about 18 biscuits, using a 5cm/2in heart-shaped cutter. Place on a heavy baking sheet and bake for about 10 minutes, until golden.

3 Leave the biscuits standing for 5 minutes to set. Using a metal spatula, transfer carefully from the baking sheet on to a wire rack to cool completely. The biscuits can be stored in an airtight container for up to one week.

Vanilla Crescents

These attractively shaped cookies are sweet and delicate, ideal for an elegant afternoon tea.

Makes 36

❧

INGREDIENTS

175g/6oz/1¼ cups unblanched almonds
115g/4oz/1 cup plain flour
pinch of salt
225g/8oz/1 cup unsalted butter
115g/4oz/½ cup granulated sugar
5ml/1 tsp vanilla essence
icing sugar for dusting

❧

1 Grind the almonds with a few tablespoons of the flour in a food processor, blender or nut grinder.

2 Sift the remaining flour with the salt into a bowl. Set aside.

3 With an electric mixer, cream together the butter and sugar until light and fluffy.

4 Add the almonds, vanilla essence and the flour mixture. Stir to mix well. Gather the dough into a ball, wrap in greaseproof paper, and chill for at least 30 minutes.

5 Preheat the oven to 160°C/325°F/ Gas 3. Lightly grease two baking sheets.

6 Break off walnut-size pieces of dough and roll into small cylinders about 1cm/½in in diameter. Bend into small crescents and place on the prepared baking sheets.

7 Bake for about 20 minutes until dry but not brown. Transfer to a wire rack to cool only slightly. Set the rack over a baking sheet and dust with an even layer of icing sugar. Leave to cool completely.

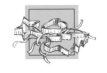

Chocolate Fruit and Nut Cookies

These simple, chunky gingerbread biscuits make a delicious gift, especially when presented in a decorative gift box. The combination of walnuts, almonds and cherries is very effective, but you can use any other mixture of glacé fruits and nuts.

Makes 20

❦

INGREDIENTS

50g/2oz/4 tbsp caster sugar
75ml/3fl oz/¹⁄₃ cup water
225g/8oz plain chocolate, chopped
40g/1¹⁄₂oz/³⁄₄ cup walnut halves
75g/3oz/¹⁄₃ cup glacé cherries, chopped into small wedges
115g/4oz/1 cup whole blanched almonds
For the Lebkuchen
115g/4oz/¹⁄₂ cup unsalted butter
115g/4oz/²⁄₃ cup light muscovado sugar
1 egg, beaten
115g/4oz/¹⁄₃ cup black treacle
400g/14oz/3¹⁄₂ cups self-raising flour
5ml/1 tsp ground ginger
2.5ml/¹⁄₂ tsp ground cloves
1.5ml/¹⁄₄ tsp chilli powder

❦

Cook's Tip Carefully stack the biscuits in a pretty box or tin, lined with tissue paper, or tie in cellophane bundles.

1 To make the lebkuchen, cream together the butter and sugar until pale and fluffy. Beat in the egg and black treacle. Sift the flour, ginger, cloves and chilli powder into the bowl. Using a wooden spoon, gradually mix the ingredients together to make a stiff paste. Turn on to a lightly floured work surface and knead lightly until smooth. Wrap and chill for 30 minutes.

2 Preheat the oven to 180°C/350°F/ Gas 4. Grease two baking sheets. Shape the dough into a roll, 20cm/8in long. Chill for 30 minutes. Cut into 20 slices and space them on the baking sheets. Bake for 10 minutes. Leave on the baking sheets for 5 minutes and then transfer to a wire rack and leave to cool.

3 Put the sugar and water in a small, heavy-based saucepan. Heat gently until the sugar dissolves. Bring to the boil and boil for 1 minute, until slightly syrupy. Leave for 3 minutes, to cool slightly, and then stir in the chocolate until it has melted and made a smooth sauce.

4 Place the wire rack of biscuits over a large tray or board. Spoon a little of the chocolate mixture over the biscuits, spreading it to the edges with the back of the spoon.

5 Gently press a walnut half into the centre of each biscuit. Arrange pieces of glacé cherry and almonds alternately around the nuts. Leave to set in a cool place.

Black-and-White Ginger Florentines

These florentines can be refrigerated in an airtight container for one week.

Makes 30

INGREDIENTS

120ml/4fl oz/¹/₂ cup double cream
50g/2oz/¹/₄ cup unsalted butter
90g/3¹/₂oz/¹/₂ cup granulated sugar
30ml/2 tbsp honey
150g/5oz/1¹/₃ cups flaked almonds
40g/1¹/₂oz/¹/₃ cup plain flour
2.5ml/¹/₂ tsp ground ginger
50g/2oz/¹/₃ cup diced candied orange peel
65g/2¹/₂oz/¹/₂ cup diced stem ginger
200g/7oz plain chocolate, chopped
150g/5oz fine quality white chocolate, chopped

3 Drop teaspoons of the mixture on to the prepared baking sheets at least 7.5cm/3in apart. Spread each round as thinly as possible with the back of the spoon. (Dip the spoon in water to prevent sticking.)

6 In a small saucepan over a very low heat, melt the remaining chocolate, stirring frequently, until smooth. Cool slightly. In the top of a double boiler over a low heat, melt the white chocolate until smooth, stirring frequently. Remove the top of double boiler from the bottom and cool for about 5 minutes, stirring occasionally until slightly thickened.

1 Preheat the oven to 180°C/350°F/ Gas 4. Lightly grease two large baking sheets. In a medium saucepan over a medium heat, stir the cream, butter, sugar and honey until the sugar dissolves. Bring the mixture to the boil, stirring constantly.

2 Remove from the heat and stir in the almonds, flour and ground ginger until well blended. Stir in the orange peel, stem ginger and 50g/2oz/¹/₃ cup chopped plain chocolate.

4 Bake in batches for 8–10 minutes, until the edges are golden brown and the biscuits are bubbling. Do not under-bake or they will be sticky, but be careful not to over-bake as they burn easily. If you wish, use a 7.5cm/3in biscuit cutter to neaten the edges of the florentines while on the baking sheet.

5 Remove the baking sheet to the wire rack to cool for 10 minutes until firm. Using a metal palette knife, carefully transfer the florentines to a wire rack to cool completely.

7 Using a small metal palette knife, spread half the florentines with the plain chocolate on the flat side of each biscuit, swirling to create a decorative surface, and place on a wire rack, chocolate side up. Spread the remaining florentines with the melted white chocolate and place on the rack, chocolate side up. Chill for 10–15 minutes to set completely.

Jewelled Christmas Trees

These cookies make an appealing gift. They look wonderful hung on a
Christmas tree or in front of a window to catch the light.

Makes 12

INGREDIENTS

175g/6oz/1½ cups plain flour
75g/3oz/⅓ cup butter, chopped
40g/1½oz/3 tbsp caster sugar
1 egg white
30ml/2 tbsp orange juice
225g/8oz coloured fruit sweets
coloured ribbons, to decorate

1 Preheat the oven to 180°C/350°F/ Gas 4. Line two baking sheets with non-stick baking paper. Sift the flour into a mixing bowl.

2 Rub the butter into the flour until the mixture resembles fine breadcrumbs. Stir in the sugar, egg white and enough orange juice to form a soft dough. Knead on a lightly floured surface until smooth.

3 Roll out thinly and stamp out as many shapes as possible using a floured Christmas tree cutter. Transfer the shapes to the prepared baking sheets, spacing them well apart. Knead the trimmings together.

4 Using a 1cm/½in round cutter or the end of a large plain piping nozzle, stamp out and remove six rounds from each tree shape. Cut each sweet into three and place a piece in each hole. Make a small hole at the top of each tree to thread through the ribbon.

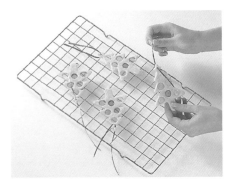

5 Bake for 15–20 minutes, until the biscuits are slightly gold in colour and the sweets have melted and filled the holes. Cool on the baking sheets. Repeat until you have used up the remaining cookie dough and sweets. Thread short lengths of ribbon through the holes so that the biscuits can be hung up.

Christmas Cookies

Makes 30

INGREDIENTS

175g/6oz/³/₄ cup unsalted butter
300g/11oz/1¹/₄ cups caster sugar
1 egg
1 egg yolk
5ml/1 tsp vanilla essence
grated rind of 1 lemon
pinch of salt
300g/11oz/2¹/₂ cups plain flour
For the decoration (optional)
coloured icing and small sweets
such as silver balls, coloured
sugar crystals

1 With an electric mixer, cream the butter until soft. Add the sugar gradually and continue beating until light and fluffy.

2 Using a wooden spoon, slowly mix in the whole egg and the egg yolk. Add the vanilla essence, lemon rind and salt. Stir to mix well.

3 Sift the flour over the mixture and stir to blend. Gather the dough into a ball, wrap, and chill for 30 minutes.

4 Preheat the oven to 190°C/375°F/ Gas 5. On a floured surface, roll out until about 3mm/¹/₈in thick.

5 Stamp out shapes or rounds with floured cookie cutters.

6 Bake for about 8 minutes until lightly coloured. Transfer to a wire rack and leave to cool completely before decorating, if wished, with icing and sweets.

Glazed Ginger Cookies

These also make good hanging biscuits for decorating trees and garlands. For this, make a hole in each biscuit with a skewer, and thread with fine ribbon.

Makes about 20

INGREDIENTS

1 quantity Golden Gingerbread mixture
2 quantities Icing Glaze
red and green food colourings
175g/6oz white almond paste

1 Preheat the oven to 180°C/350°F/Gas 4. Grease a large baking sheet. Roll out the gingerbread dough on a floured surface and, using a selection of floured cookie cutters, cut out a variety of shapes, such as trees, stars, crescents and bells. Transfer to the prepared baking sheet and bake for 8–10 minutes, until just beginning to colour around the edges. Leave the cookies on the baking sheet for 3 minutes.

2 Transfer the cookies to a wire rack and leave to cool. Place the wire rack over a large tray or plate. Using a dessertspoon, spoon the icing glaze over the cookies until they are completely covered. Leave in a cool place to dry for several hours.

3 Knead red food colouring into half of the almond paste and green into the other half. Roll a thin length of each coloured paste and then twist the two together into a rope.

4 Secure a rope of paste around a biscuit, dampening the icing with a little water, if necessary, to hold it in place. Repeat on about half of the cookies. Dilute a little of each food colouring with water. Using a fine paintbrush, paint festive decorations over the plain cookies. Leave to dry and then wrap in tissue paper.

Festive and Fancy Cookies

Easter Cookies

These are enjoyed as a traditional part of the Christian festival of Easter.

Makes 16–18

❦

INGREDIENTS

115g/4oz/¹/₂ cup butter, chopped
75g/3oz/¹/₃ cup caster sugar, plus
extra for sprinkling
1 egg, separated
200g/7oz/1³/₄ cups plain four
2.5ml/¹/₂ tsp ground mixed spice
2.5ml/¹/₂ tsp ground cinnamon
50g/2oz/scant ¹/₃ cup currants
15ml/1 tbsp chopped mixed peel
15–30ml/1–2 tbsp milk

❦

3 Turn the dough on to a floured surface, knead lightly until just smooth, then roll out using a floured rolling pin, to about 5mm/¹/₄in thick. Cut the dough into rounds using a 5cm/2in fluted biscuit cutter. Transfer the rounds to the prepared baking sheets and bake for 10 minutes.

4 Beat the egg white, then brush over the biscuits. Sprinkle with caster sugar and return to the oven for a further 10 minutes, until golden. Transfer to a wire rack to cool.

1 Preheat the oven to 200°C/400°F/ Gas 6. Lightly grease two baking sheets. Beat together the butter and sugar, then beat in the egg yolk.

2 Sift the flour and spices over the egg mixture, then fold in with the currants and peel, adding sufficient milk to mix to a fairly soft dough.

Sultana Cornmeal Cookies

These little yellow biscuits come from the Veneto region of Italy.

Makes 48

INGREDIENTS

75g/3oz/¹/₂ cup sultanas
*115g/4oz/1 cup finely ground
yellow cornmeal*
175g/6oz/1¹/₂ cups plain flour
7.5ml/1¹/₂ tsp baking powder
pinch of salt
225g/8oz/1 cup butter
225g/8oz/1 cup granulated sugar
2 eggs
*15ml/1 tbsp marsala or 5ml/1 tsp
vanilla essence*

1 Soak the sultanas in a small bowl of warm water for 15 minutes. Drain. Preheat the oven to 180°C/ 350°F/Gas 4. Grease a baking sheet.

2 Sift the cornmeal, flour, baking powder and salt together into a mixing bowl. Set aside.

3 Cream the butter and sugar until light and fluffy. Beat in the eggs, one at a time. Beat in the marsala or vanilla essence.

4 Add the dry ingredients to the butter mixture, beating until well blended. Stir in the sultanas.

5 Drop heaped teaspoons of the mixture on to the prepared baking sheet in rows about 5cm/2in apart. Bake for 7–8 minutes, until the cookies are golden brown at the edges. Transfer to a wire rack to cool.

Amaretti

If bitter almonds are not available, make up the weight with sweet almonds.

Makes 36

INGREDIENTS

150g/5oz/1¹/₄ cups sweet almonds
50g/2oz/¹/₂ cup bitter almonds
225g/8oz/1 cup caster sugar
2 egg whites
*2.5ml/¹/₂ tsp almond essence or
5ml/1 tsp vanilla essence*
icing sugar for dusting

1 Preheat the oven to 160°C/325°F/ Gas 3. Peel the almonds by dropping them into a saucepan of boiling water for 1–2 minutes. Drain. Rub the almonds in a cloth to remove the skins.

2 Place the almonds on a baking tray and let them dry out in the oven for 10–15 minutes without browning. Remove from the oven and allow to cool. Turn the oven off. Dust with flour.

3 Grind the almonds with half of the sugar in a food processor. Use an electric beater or wire whisk to beat the egg whites until they form soft peaks.

4 Sprinkle over half the remaining sugar and continue beating until stiff peaks are formed. Gently fold in the remaining sugar, the almond or vanilla essence and the almonds.

5 Spoon the almond mixture into a piping bag fitted with a smooth nozzle. Pipe out the mixture in rounds the size of a walnut. Sprinkle lightly with the icing sugar, and leave to stand for 2 hours. Near the end of this time, turn the oven on again and preheat to 180°C/350°F/Gas 4.

6 Bake for 15 minutes, until pale gold. Remove from the oven and cool on a wire rack.

Decorated Chocolate Lebkuchen

Wrapped in paper or cellophane, or beautifully boxed, these decorated cookies make a lovely present. Don't make them too far in advance as the chocolate will gradually discolour.

Makes 40

INGREDIENTS

*1 quantity Lebkuchen mixture
115g/4oz plain chocolate,
chopped
115g/4oz milk chocolate, chopped
115g/4oz white chocolate,
chopped
chocolate vermicelli, for
sprinkling
cocoa powder or icing sugar for
dusting*

1 Grease two baking sheets. Roll out just over half of the Lebkuchen mixture until 5mm/¼in thick. Cut out heart shapes, using a 4.5cm/1¼in heart-shaped cutter. Transfer to baking sheet. Gather the trimmings together with the remaining dough and cut into 20 pieces. Roll into balls and place on the baking sheet. Flatten each ball slightly with your fingers.

2 Chill both sheets for 30 minutes. Preheat the oven to 180°C/350°F/Gas 4. Bake for 8–10 minutes. Cool on a wire rack.

3 Melt the plain chocolate in a heatproof bowl over a small saucepan of hot water. Melt the milk and white chocolate in separate bowls.

4 Make three small paper piping bags out of greaseproof paper. Spoon a little of each chocolate into the three paper piping bags and reserve. Spoon a little plain chocolate over one third of the biscuits, spreading it slightly to cover them completely. (Tapping the rack gently will help the chocolate to run down the sides.)

5 Snip the merest tip from the bag of white chocolate and drizzle it over some of the coated biscuits, to give a decorative finish.

6 Sprinkle the chocolate vermicelli over the plain chocolate-coated biscuits that haven't been decorated. Coat the remaining biscuits with the milk and white chocolate and decorate some of these with more chocolate from the piping bags, contrasting the colours. Scatter more undecorated biscuits with vermicelli. Leave the biscuits to set.

7 Transfer the undecorated biscuits to a plate or tray and dust lightly with cocoa powder or icing sugar.

Cook's Tip If the chocolate in the bowls starts to set before you have finished decorating, put the bowls back over the heat for 1–2 minutes. If the chocolate in the piping bags starts to harden, microwave briefly or put in a clean bowl over a pan of simmering water until soft.

Macaroons

Freshly ground almonds, lightly toasted beforehand to intensify the flavour,

give these biscuits their rich taste and texture so, for best results,

avoid using ready-ground almonds as a shortcut.

Makes 12

INGREDIENTS

*115g/4oz/1½ cup blanched
almonds, toasted
165g/5½oz/¾ cup caster sugar
2 egg whites
2.5ml/½ tsp almond or vanilla
essence
icing sugar for dusting*

1 Preheat the oven to 180°C/350°F/ Gas 4. Line a large baking sheet with non-stick baking paper. Reserve 12 almonds for decorating. In a food processor grind the rest of the almonds with the sugar.

2 With the machine running, slowly pour in enough of the egg whites to form a soft dough. Add the almond or vanilla essence and pulse to mix.

3 With moistened hands, shape the mixture into walnut-size balls and arrange on the baking sheet.

4 Press one of the reserved almonds on to each ball, flattening them slightly, and dust lightly with icing sugar. Bake for about 10–12 minutes, until the tops are golden and feel slightly firm. Transfer to a wire rack, cool slightly, then peel the biscuits off the paper and leave to cool completely.

Cook's Tip To toast the almonds, spread them on a baking sheet and bake in the preheated oven for 10–15 minutes, until golden. Leave to cool before grinding.

Madeleines

These little tea cakes, baked in a special tin with shell-shaped cups,

were made famous by Marcel Proust, who referred to them in his novel.

They are best eaten on the day they are made.

Makes 12

INGREDIENTS

*165g/5½oz/1¼ cups plain flour
5ml/1 tsp baking powder
2 eggs
75g/3oz/¾ cup icing sugar, plus
extra for dusting
grated rind of 1 lemon or orange
15ml/1 tbsp lemon or orange juice
75g/3oz/6 tbsp unsalted butter,
melted and slightly cooled*

1 Preheat the oven to 190°C/375°F/ Gas 5. Generously butter a 12-cup madeleine tin. Sift together the flour and baking powder.

2 Using an electric mixer, beat the eggs and icing sugar for 5–7 minutes until thick and creamy and the mixture forms a ribbon when the beaters are lifted. Gently fold in the lemon or orange rind and juice.

3 Beginning with the flour mixture, alternately fold in the flour and melted butter in four batches. Leave the mixture to stand for 10 minutes, then carefully spoon into the tin. Tap gently to release any air bubbles.

4 Bake for 12–15 minutes, rotating the tin halfway through cooking, until a skewer or cake tester inserted in the centre comes out clean. Tip on to a wire rack to cool completely and dust with icing sugar before serving.

Cook's Tip If you don't have a special tin for making madeleines, you can use a bun tin, preferably with a non-stick coating. The cakes won't have the characteristic ridges and shell shape, but they are quite pretty dusted with a little icing sugar.

Tuiles d'Amandes

These biscuits are named after the French roof tiles they so resemble. Making them is a little fiddly, so bake only four at a time until you get the knack. With a little practice you will find them easy.

Makes 24

INGREDIENTS

65g/2¹/₂oz/generous ¹/₂ cup whole blanched almonds, lightly toasted
65g/2¹/₂oz/¹/₃ cup caster sugar
40g/1¹/₂oz/3 tbsp unsalted butter
2 egg whites
2.5ml/¹/₂ tsp almond essence
30g/1¹/₄oz/scant ¹/₄ cup plain flour, sifted
50g/2oz/¹/₂ cup flaked almonds

Cook's Tip If the biscuits flatten or lose their crispness, reheat them on a baking sheet in a moderate oven, until completely flat, then reshape.

1 Preheat the oven to 200°C/400°F/ Gas 6. Generously butter two heavy baking sheets.

2 Place the almonds and about 30ml/2 tbsp of the sugar in a food processor fitted with the metal blade and process until finely ground.

3 Beat the butter until creamy, then add the remaining sugar and beat until light and fluffy. Gradually beat in the egg whites, then add the almond essence. Sift the flour over the butter mixture, fold in, then fold in the ground almond mixture.

4 Drop tablespoonfuls of the mixture on to the prepared baking sheets about 15cm/6in apart. With the back of a wet spoon, spread each mound into a paper-thin 7.5cm/3in round. (Don't worry if holes appear, they will fill in.) Sprinkle with flaked almonds.

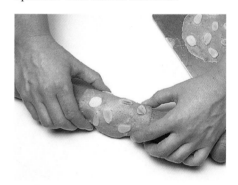

5 Bake the cookies, one sheet at a time, for 5–6 minutes, until the edges are golden and the centres still pale. Working quickly, use a thin palette knife to loosen the edges of one cookie. Lift the cookie on the palette knife and place over a rolling pin, then press down the sides of the biscuit to curve it.

6 Continue shaping the cookies, transferring them to a wire rack as they cool. If they become too crisp to shape, return the baking sheet to the hot oven for 15–30 seconds, then continue as above.

Flaked Almond Biscuits

Makes 30

INGREDIENTS

175g/6oz/³/₄ cup butter or
margarine, chopped
225g/8oz/2 cups self-raising flour
150g/5oz/²/₃ cup caster sugar
2.5ml/¹/₂ tsp ground cinnamon
1 egg, separated
30ml/2 tbsp cold water
50g/2oz/¹/₂ cup flaked almonds

1 Preheat the oven to 180°C/350°F/ Gas 4. Rub the butter or margarine into the flour. Reserve 15ml/1 tbsp of the sugar and mix the rest with the cinnamon. Stir into the flour and then add the egg yolk and cold water and mix to a firm dough.

2 Roll out the dough on a lightly floured board to 1cm/¹/₂in thick. Sprinkle over the almonds. Continue rolling until the dough is approximately 5mm/¹/₄in thick.

3 Using a floured fluted round cutter, cut the dough into rounds. Use a palette knife to lift them on to an ungreased baking sheet. Re-form the dough and cut more rounds to use all the dough. Whisk the egg white lightly, brush it over the cookies, and sprinkle over the remaining sugar.

4 Bake for about 10–15 minutes, until golden. To remove, slide a palette knife under the cookies, which will still seem a bit soft, but they harden as they cool. Leave on a wire rack until quite cold.

Mocha Viennese Swirls

Makes 20

INGREDIENTS

*250g/9oz plain chocolate,
chopped
200g/7oz/scant 1 cup unsalted
butter
50g/2oz/¹/₂ cup icing sugar
30ml/2 tbsp strong black coffee
200g/7oz/1³/₄ cups plain flour
50g/2oz/¹/₂ cup cornflour
about 20 blanched almonds*

Cook's Tip If the mixture is too stiff to pipe, soften it with a little more black coffee.

1 Preheat the oven to 190°C/375°F/ Gas 5. Lightly grease two large baking sheets. Melt 115g/4oz of the chocolate in a heatproof bowl over a saucepan of hot water. Cream the butter with the icing sugar in a bowl until smooth and pale. Beat in the melted chocolate, then the strong black coffee.

2 Sift the flour and cornflour over the mixture. Fold in lightly and evenly to make a soft mixture.

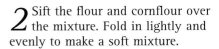

3 Spoon the mixture into a piping bag fitted with a large star nozzle and pipe 20 swirls on the prepared baking sheets, allowing room for spreading during baking.

4 Press an almond into the centre of each swirl. Bake for about 15 minutes, until the biscuits are firm and just beginning to brown. Leave to cool for about 10 minutes on the baking sheets, then lift carefully on to a wire rack to cool completely.

5 Melt the remaining chocolate and dip the base of each swirl to coat. Place on a sheet of non-stick baking paper and leave to set.

Chocolate Amaretti

Makes 24

INGREDIENTS

150g/5oz/1¼ cups blanched whole almonds
90g/3½oz/scant ½ cup caster sugar
15ml/1 tbsp cocoa powder
30ml/2 tbsp icing sugar
2 egg whites
pinch of cream of tartar
5ml/1 tsp almond essence
flaked almonds, to decorate

1 Preheat the oven to 180°C/350°F/ Gas 4. Place the almonds on a baking sheet and bake for 10– 12 minutes until golden brown. Leave to cool. Reduce the oven temperature to 160°C/325°F/Gas 3. Line a large baking sheet with non-stick baking paper. In a food processor, process the almonds with half the sugar until they are finely ground but not oily. Transfer to a bowl and sift in the cocoa and icing sugar. Set aside.

2 In a mixing bowl with an electric mixer, beat the egg whites and cream of tartar until stiff peaks form. Sprinkle in the remaining sugar a tablespoon at a time, beating well after each addition, and continue beating until the whites are glossy and stiff. Beat in the almond essence.

3 Sprinkle over the almond-sugar mixture and gently fold into the beaten egg whites until just blended. Spoon the mixture into a large piping bag fitted with a plain 1cm/½in nozzle. Pipe 4cm/1½in rounds about 2.5cm/1in apart on the prepared baking sheet. Press a flaked almond into the centre of each.

4 Bake the cookies for 12–15 minutes, or until crisp. Remove the baking sheets to a wire rack to cool for 10 minutes. With a metal palette knife, remove the amarettis to a wire rack to cool completely.

Nut Lace Cookies

Makes 18

INGREDIENTS

50g/2oz/¹/₂ cup blanched almonds
50g/2oz/4 tbsp butter
45ml/3 tbsp plain flour
115g/4oz/¹/₂ cup granulated sugar
30ml/2 tbsp double cream
2.5ml/¹/₂ tsp vanilla essence

Variation Add 40g/1¹/₂oz/¹/₄ cup finely chopped candied orange peel to the mixture.

1 Preheat the oven to 190°C/375°F/ Gas 5. Grease 1–2 baking sheets.

2 With a sharp knife, chop the almonds as finely as possible. Alternatively, use a food processor, blender or nut grinder to chop the nuts very finely.

3 Melt the butter in a small saucepan over a low heat. Remove from the heat and stir in the remaining ingredients, including the almonds.

4 Drop teaspoonfuls of the mixture 6cm/2¹/₂in apart on the prepared baking sheets. Bake for about 5 minutes until golden. Cool on the sheets briefly, until the cookies are just stiff enough to lift off.

5 With a metal spatula, transfer the cookies to a wire rack to cool completely.

Oatmeal Lace Cookies

Makes 36

INGREDIENTS

165g/5¹/₂oz/²/₃ cup butter or margarine
175g/6oz/1¹/₂ cups rolled oats
175g/6oz/³/₄ cup firmly packed dark brown sugar
175g/6oz/³/₄ cup granulated sugar
45ml/3 tbsp plain flour
pinch of salt
1 egg, lightly beaten
5ml/1 tsp vanilla essence
50g/2oz/¹/₂ cup pecans or walnuts, finely chopped

1 Preheat the oven to 180°C/350°F/ Gas 4. Grease two baking sheets.

2 Melt the butter or margarine in a small saucepan over a low heat. Set aside.

3 In a mixing bowl, combine the oats, brown sugar, granulated sugar, flour and salt.

4 Add the butter or margarine, the egg and vanilla essence.

5 Mix until blended, then stir in the chopped nuts.

6 Drop rounded teaspoonfuls of the batter about 5cm/2in apart on the prepared baking sheets. Bake for 5–8 minutes until lightly browned on the edges and bubbling. Leave to cool for 2 minutes, then transfer to a wire rack to cool completely.

Raspberry Sandwich Cookies

Children will love these sweet, sticky treats.

Makes 32

INGREDIENTS

115g/4oz/1 cup blanched almonds
175g/6oz/1½ cups plain flour
175g/6oz/¾ cup butter
115g/4oz/½ cup caster sugar
grated rind of 1 lemon
5ml/1 tsp vanilla essence
1 egg white
pinch of salt
40g/1½oz/⅓ cup slivered
almonds, chopped
350g/12oz/1 cup raspberry jam
15ml/1 tbsp lemon juice

1 Finely grind the almonds and 45ml/3 tbsp of the flour.

2 Cream together the butter and sugar until light and fluffy. Stir in the lemon rind and vanilla essence. Add the ground almonds and remaining flour and mix well to form a dough. Gather into a ball, wrap in greaseproof paper, and chill for 1 hour. Preheat the oven to 160°C/325°F/Gas 3. Line two baking sheets with greaseproof paper.

3 Divide the dough into four. Roll each piece out on a lightly floured surface to a thickness of 3mm/⅛in. With a floured 6cm/2½in pastry cutter, stamp out circles, then stamp out the centres from half the circles.

4 When all the dough has been used, check you have equal numbers of rings and circles, then place the dough rings and circles 1cm/½in apart on the prepared baking sheets.

5 Whisk the egg white with the salt until just frothy. Brush only the cookie rings with the egg white, then sprinkle over the chopped almonds. Bake for 12–15 minutes until very lightly browned. Leave to cool for a few minutes on the sheets before transferring to a wire rack.

6 In a saucepan, melt the jam with the lemon juice until it comes to a simmer. Brush the jam over the cookie circles and sandwich together with the rings. Store in an airtight container with sheets of greaseproof paper between the layers.

Chocolate Marzipan Cookies

These crisp little cookies satisfy a sweet tooth and have a little almond surprise inside.

Makes 36

INGREDIENTS

200g/7oz/scant 1 cup unsalted butter
200g/7oz/generous 1 cup light muscovado sugar
1 egg
300g/11oz/2½ cups plain flour
60ml/4 tbsp cocoa powder
200g/7oz white almond paste
115g/4oz white chocolate, chopped

1 Preheat the oven to 190°C/375°F/ Gas 5. Lightly grease two large baking sheets. Cream the butter with the sugar in a bowl until pale and fluffy. Add the egg and beat well.

2 Sift the flour and cocoa over the mixture. Stir in, first with a wooden spoon, then with clean hands, pressing the mixture together to make a fairly soft dough.

3 Roll out about half the dough on a lightly floured surface to a thickness of about 5mm/¼in. Using a 5cm/2in biscuit cutter, cut out rounds, re-rolling the dough as required until you have about 36 rounds.

4 Cut the almond paste into about 36 equal pieces. Roll into balls, flatten slightly and place one on each round of dough. Roll out the remaining dough, cut out more rounds, then place on top of the almond paste. Press the dough edges to seal. Bake for 10–12 minutes until the cookies have risen well. Cool completely. Melt the white chocolate, spoon into a paper piping bag and pipe on to the biscuits.

Cook's Tip If the dough is too sticky to roll, chill it for about 30 minutes, then try again.

Lady Fingers

Named after the pale, slim fingers of highborn gentlewomen.

Makes 18

INGREDIENTS

90g/3¹/₂oz/²/₃ cup plain flour
pinch of salt
4 eggs, separated
115g/4oz/¹/₂ cup granulated sugar
2.5ml/¹/₂ tsp vanilla essence
icing sugar for sprinkling

 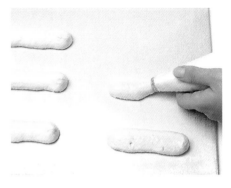

1 Preheat the oven to 150°C/300°F/ Gas 2. Grease two baking sheets, then coat lightly with flour, and shake off the excess.

2 Sift the flour and salt together twice.

3 With an electric mixer, beat the egg yolks with half of the sugar until thick enough to leave a ribbon trail when the beaters are lifted.

4 In another bowl, beat the egg whites until stiff. Beat in the remaining sugar until glossy.

5 Sift the flour over the yolks and spoon a large dollop of egg whites over the flour. Carefully fold in with a large metal spoon, adding the vanilla essence. Gently fold in the remaining whites.

6 Spoon the mixture into a piping bag fitted with a large plain nozzle. Pipe 10cm/4in long lines on the prepared baking sheets about 2.5cm/1in apart. Sift over a layer of icing sugar. Turn the sheet upside down to dislodge any excess sugar.

7 Bake for about 20 minutes until crusty on the outside but soft in the centre. Cool slightly on the baking sheets before transferring to a wire rack.

Walnut Cookies

Makes 60

INGREDIENTS

115g/4oz/¹/₂ cup butter or margarine
175g/6oz/³/₄ cup caster sugar
115g/4oz/1 cup plain flour
10ml/2 tsp vanilla essence
115g/4oz/1 cup walnuts, finely chopped

1 Preheat the oven to 150°C/300°F/ Gas 2. Grease two baking sheets.

2 With an electric mixer, cream the butter or margarine until soft. Add 50g/2oz/¹/₄ cup of the sugar and continue beating until light and fluffy. Stir in the flour, vanilla essence and walnuts. Drop teaspoonfuls of the batter 2.5–5cm/1–2in apart on the prepared baking sheets and flatten slightly. Bake for about 25 minutes.

3 Transfer to a wire rack set over a baking sheet and sprinkle with the remaining sugar.

Variation To make Almond Cookies, use an equal amount of finely chopped unblanched almonds instead of walnuts. Replace half the vanilla with 2.5ml/¹/₂ tsp almond essence.

Cookies
for Kids

Lemony Peanut Pairs

For those who don't like peanut butter, use buttercream or chocolate-and-nut spread instead.

Makes 8–10

INGREDIENTS

*40g/1¹/₂oz/¹/₄ cup soft light brown
sugar
50g/2oz/¹/₄ cup soft margarine
5ml/1 tsp grated lemon rind
75g/3oz/³/₄ cup wholemeal flour
50g/2oz/¹/₄ cup chopped
crystallised pineapple
25g/1oz/2 tbsp smooth peanut
butter
sifted icing sugar for dusting*

1 Preheat the oven to 190°C/375°F/
Gas 3. Grease a baking sheet.
Cream the sugar, margarine and
lemon rind together. Work in the
flour and knead until smooth.

2 Roll out thinly and cut into
rounds, then place on the baking
sheet. Press on pieces of pineapple
and bake for 15–20 minutes. Cool.
Sandwich together with peanut
butter, dust with icing sugar.

Ginger Cookies

If your children enjoy cooking with you, mixing and rolling the dough, or cutting out

different shapes, this is the ideal recipe to let them practise on.

Makes 16

INGREDIENTS

*115g/4oz/²/₃ cup soft brown sugar
115g/4oz/¹/₂ cup soft margarine
pinch of salt
few drops of vanilla essence
175g/6oz/1¹/₄ cups wholemeal
plain flour
15g/¹/₂oz/1 tbsp cocoa, sifted
10ml/2 tsp ground ginger
a little milk
glacé icing and glacé cherries, to
decorate*

1 Preheat the oven to 190°C/375°F/
Gas 5. Grease a baking sheet.
Cream together the sugar, margarine,
salt and vanilla essence until very
soft and light.

2 Work in the flour, cocoa and
ginger, adding a little milk, if
necessary, to bind the mixture. Knead
lightly on a floured surface until
smooth.

3 Roll out the dough to about
5mm/¹/₄in thick. Stamp out shapes
using floured biscuit cutters and place
on the prepared baking sheet.

4 Bake the cookies for 10–
15 minutes. Leave to cool on the
baking sheets until firm, then transfer
to a wire rack to cool completely.
Decorate with glacé icing and glacé
cherries.

Fruit and Nut Clusters

This is a fun no-cook recipe which children will like.

Makes 24

INGREDIENTS

225g/8oz white chocolate
50g/2oz/¹/₃ cup sunflower seeds
50g/2oz/¹/₂ cup almond slivers
50g/2oz/¹/₃ cup sesame seeds
50g/2oz/¹/₃ cup seedless raisins
5ml/1 tsp ground cinnamon

1 Break the white chocolate into small pieces. Put the chocolate into a heatproof bowl over a saucepan of hot water on a low heat. Do not allow the water to touch the base of the bowl, or the chocolate may become too hot.

2 Alternatively, put the chocolate in a microwave-proof container and heat it on Medium for 3 minutes. Stir the melted chocolate until it is smooth and glossy.

3 Mix the remaining ingredients together, pour on the chocolate and stir well.

4 Using a teaspoon, spoon the mixture into paper cases and leave to set.

Marshmallow Crispie Cakes

Makes 45

INGREDIENTS

250g/9oz bag of toffees
50g/2oz/4 tbsp butter
45ml/3 tbsp milk
115g/4oz/1 cup marshmallows
175g/6oz/6 cups Rice Crispies

1 Lightly brush a 20 x 33cm/8 x 13in roasting tin with a little oil. Put the toffees, butter and milk in a saucepan and heat gently, stirring until the toffees have melted.

2 Add the marshmallows and cereal and stir until well mixed and the marshmallows have melted.

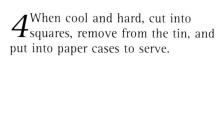

3 Spoon the mixture into the prepared roasting tin, level the surface and leave to set.

4 When cool and hard, cut into squares, remove from the tin, and put into paper cases to serve.

Gingerbread Jungle

Snappy biscuits in animal shapes, which can be decorated in your own style.

Makes 14

INGREDIENTS

*175g/6oz/1¹/₂ cups self-raising
flour
2.5ml/¹/₂ tsp bicarbonate of soda
2.5ml/¹/₂ tsp ground cinnamon
10ml/2 tsp caster sugar
50g/2oz/¹/₄ cup butter
45ml/3 tbsp golden syrup
50g/2oz/¹/₂ cup icing sugar
5–10ml/1–2 tsp water*

Cook's Tip Any cutters can be used
with the same mixture. Obviously, the
smaller the cutters, the more biscuits
you will make.

1 Preheat the oven to 190°C/375°F/
Gas 5. Lightly oil two baking
sheets.

2 Put the flour, bicarbonate of soda,
cinnamon and caster sugar in a
bowl and mix together. Melt the
butter and syrup in a saucepan. Pour
over the dry ingredients.

3 Mix together well and then use
your hands to pull the mixture
together to make a dough.

4 Turn on to a lightly floured
surface and roll out to about
5mm/¹/₄in thick.

5 Use floured animal cutters to cut
shapes from the dough and
arrange on the prepared baking
sheets, leaving enough room between
them to rise.

6 Press the trimmings back into a
ball, roll it out and cut more
shapes. Continue until all the dough
is used. Bake for 8–12 minutes, until
lightly browned.

7 Leave to cool slightly, before
transferring to a wire rack with a
palette knife. Sift the icing sugar into
a small bowl and add enough water
to make a fairly soft icing.

8 Spoon the icing into a piping bag
fitted with a small, plain nozzle
and pipe decorations on the cookies.

Chocolate Crackle-tops

Older children will enjoy making these distinctive cookies.

Makes 38

❧

INGREDIENTS

*200g/7oz plain chocolate,
chopped
90g/3½oz/scant ½ cup unsalted
butter
115g/4oz/½ cup caster sugar
3 eggs
5ml/1 tsp vanilla essence
215g/7½oz/scant 2 cups plain
flour
25g/1oz/¼ cup unsweetened cocoa
2.5ml/½ tsp baking powder
pinch of salt
175g/6oz/1½ cups icing sugar for
coating*

❧

1 In a medium saucepan over a low heat, melt the chocolate and butter together until smooth, stirring frequently.

2 Remove from the heat. Stir in the sugar, and continue stirring for 2–3 minutes, until the sugar dissolves. Add the eggs one at a time, beating well after each addition; stir in the vanilla.

3 Into a bowl, sift together the flour, cocoa, baking powder and salt. Gradually stir into the chocolate mixture in batches, until just blended.

4 Cover the dough and refrigerate for at least 1 hour, until the dough is cold and holds its shape.

5 Preheat the oven to 160°C/325°F/ Gas 3. Grease two or more large baking sheets. Place the icing sugar in a small, deep bowl. Using a small ice-cream scoop or round teaspoon, scoop cold dough into small balls and, between the palms of your hands, roll into 4cm/1½in balls.

6 Drop each ball into the icing sugar and roll until heavily coated. Remove with a slotted spoon and tap against the side of the bowl to remove excess sugar. Place on the prepared baking sheets 4cm/1½in apart.

7 Bake the cookies for 10– 15 minutes, until the tops feel slightly firm when touched. Remove the baking sheet to a wire rack for 2–3 minutes. With a metal palette knife, remove the cookies to a wire rack to cool completely.

Chocolate Dominoes

A recipe for children to eat rather than make. Ideal for birthday parties.

Makes 16

❧

INGREDIENTS

175g/6oz/³/₄ cup soft margarine
175g/6oz/³/₄ cup caster sugar
150g/5oz/1¹/₄ cups self-raising
flour
25g/1oz/¹/₄ cup cocoa powder,
sifted
3 eggs
For the topping
175g/6oz/³/₄ cup butter
25g/1oz/¹/₄ cup cocoa powder
300g/11oz/2¹/₂ cups icing sugar
a few liquorice strips and
115g/4oz packet M & M's, for
decoration

❧

Variation To make Traffic Light Cakes, omit the cocoa and add an extra 25g/1oz/3 tbsp plain flour. Omit cocoa from the icing and add an extra 25g/1oz/4 tbsp icing sugar and 2.5ml/¹/₂ tsp vanilla essence. Spread over the cakes and decorate with red, yellow and green glacé cherries to look like traffic lights.

1 Preheat the oven to 180°C/350°F/Gas 4. Lightly brush an 18 x 28cm/7 x 11in baking tin with a little oil and line the base of the tin with greaseproof paper.

2 Put all the cake ingredients in a bowl and beat until smooth.

3 Spoon into the prepared cake tin and level the surface with a palette knife.

4 Bake for 30 minutes, until the cake springs back when pressed with the fingertips.

5 Cool in the tin for 5 minutes, then loosen the edges with a knife and transfer to a wire rack. Peel off the paper and leave the cake to cool. Turn the cake on to a chopping board and cut into 16 bars.

6 To make the topping, place the butter in a bowl, sift in the cocoa and icing sugar and beat until smooth. Spread the topping evenly over the cakes with a palette knife.

7 Add a strip of liquorice to each cake, decorate with M & M's for domino dots and arrange the cakes on a serving plate.

Gingerbread Teddies

These endearing teddies, dressed in striped pyjamas, would make a perfect gift for friends of any age. If you can't get a large cutter, make smaller teddies or use a traditional gingerbread-man cutter. You might need some help from an adult for the decorating.

Makes 6

🌿

INGREDIENTS

75g/3oz white chocolate, chopped
175g/6oz ready-to-roll white sugar paste
blue food colouring
25g/1oz plain or milk chocolate
For the gingerbread
175g/6oz/1½ cups plain flour
1.5ml/¼ tsp bicarbonate of soda
pinch of salt
5ml/1 tsp ground ginger
5ml/1 tsp ground cinnamon
65g/2½oz/⅓ cup unsalted butter, chopped
75g/3oz/⅓ cup caster sugar
30ml/2 tbsp maple or golden syrup
1 egg yolk, beaten

🌿

1 To make the gingerbread, sift together the flour, bicarbonate of soda, salt and spices into a large bowl. Rub the butter into the flour until the mixture resembles fine breadcrumbs.

2 Stir in the sugar, syrup and egg yolk and mix to a firm dough. Knead lightly. Wrap and chill for 30 minutes.

3 Preheat the oven to 180°C/350°F/ Gas 4. Grease two large baking sheets. Roll out the gingerbread dough on a floured surface and cut out teddies, using a floured 13cm/5in cookie cutter.

4 Transfer to the prepared baking sheets and bake for 10–15 minutes, until just beginning to colour around the edges. Leave on the baking sheets for 3 minutes and then transfer to a wire rack.

5 Melt half of the white chocolate. Put in a paper piping bag and snip off the tip. Make a neat template for the teddies' clothes: draw an outline of the cutter on to paper, finishing at the neck, halfway down the arms and around the legs.

6 Thinly roll the sugar paste on a surface dusted with icing sugar. Use the template to cut out the clothes, and secure them to the biscuits with the melted chocolate.

7 Use the sugar paste trimmings to add ears, eyes and snouts. Dilute the blue colouring with a little water and use it to paint the striped pyjamas.

8 Melt the remaining white chocolate and the plain or milk chocolate in separate bowls over saucepans of hot water. Put in separate paper piping bags and snip off the tips. Use the white chocolate to pipe a decorative outline around the pyjamas and use the plain or milk chocolate to pipe the faces.

Sweet Necklaces

These are too fiddly for young children to make but ideal as novelty Christmas presents.

Arrange in a pretty, tissue-lined box or tin for presentation.

Makes 12

❦

INGREDIENTS

1 quantity Lebkuchen mixture
1 quantity Royal Icing
pink food colouring
selection of small sweets
6m/6 yards fine pink, blue or
white ribbon

❦

1 Preheat the oven to 180°C/350°F/ Gas 4. Grease two large baking sheets. Roll out slightly more than half of the Lebkuchen mixture on a lightly floured surface to a thickness of 5mm/¼in.

2 Cut out stars using a floured 2.5cm/1in star cutter. Transfer to a baking sheet, spacing them evenly. Taking care not to distort the shape of the stars, make a large hole in the centre of each, using a metal or wooden skewer.

3 Gather the trimmings together with the remaining dough. Roll the dough under the palms of your hands, to make a thick sausage about 2.5cm/1in in diameter. Cut in 1cm/½in slices. Using the skewer, make a hole in the centre of each. Put on the second baking sheet.

4 Bake for about 8 minutes, until slightly risen and just beginning to colour. Remove from the oven and, while still warm, re-make the skewer holes as the gingerbread will have spread slightly during baking. Leave to cool on a wire rack.

5 Put half the royal icing in a paper piping bag and snip off a tip. Use to pipe outlines around the stars. Colour the remaining icing with the pink colouring. Spoon into a paper piping bag fitted with a star nozzle.

6 Cut the sweets into smaller pieces and use to decorate the biscuits. Leave to harden.

7 Cut the ribbon into 50cm/20in lengths. Thread a selection of the biscuits on to each ribbon.

Choc-tipped Cookies

Get those cold hands wrapped round a steaming hot drink,

and tuck into choc-tipped cookies.

Makes 22

INGREDIENTS

115g/4oz/¹/₂ cup margarine
45ml/3 tbsp icing sugar, sifted
150g/5oz/1¹/₄ cups plain flour
few drops vanilla essence
75g/3oz plain chocolate, chopped

1 Preheat the oven to 180°C/350°F/ Gas 4. Lightly grease two baking sheets. Put the margarine and icing sugar in a bowl and cream them together until very soft. Mix in the flour and vanilla essence.

2 Spoon the mixture into a large piping bag fitted with a large star nozzle and pipe 10–13cm/4–5in lines on the prepared baking sheets. Cook for 15–20 minutes, until pale golden brown. Leave to cool slightly before lifting on to a wire rack. Leave the biscuits to cool completely.

3 Put the chocolate in a small heatproof bowl. Stand in a saucepan of hot, but not boiling, water and leave to melt. Dip both ends of each biscuit into the chocolate, put back on the rack and leave to set. Serve with hot chocolate topped with whipped cream.

Cook's Tip Make round biscuits if you prefer, and dip half of each biscuit in the melted chocolate.

Five-spice Fingers

Light, crumbly biscuits with an unusual Chinese five-spice flavouring.

Makes 28

❦

INGREDIENTS

115g/4oz/¹/₂ cup margarine
50g/2oz/¹/₂ cup icing sugar
115g/4oz/1 cup plain flour
10ml/2 tsp five-spice powder
grated rind and juice of ¹/₂ orange

❦

1 Preheat the oven to 180°C/
350°F/Gas 4. Lightly grease
two baking sheets. Put the margarine
and half the icing sugar in a bowl
and beat with a wooden spoon, until
the mixture is smooth and creamy.

2 Add the flour and five-spice
powder and beat again. Spoon
the mixture into a large piping bag
fitted with a large star nozzle.

3 Pipe short lines of mixture, about
7.5cm/3in long, on the prepared
baking sheets. Leave enough room for
them to spread.

4 Bake for 15 minutes, until lightly
browned. Leave to cool slightly,
before transferring to a wire rack
with a palette knife.

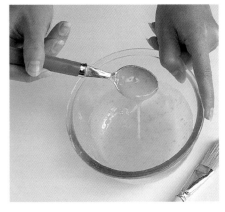

5 Sift the remaining icing sugar
into a small bowl and stir in the
orange rind. Add enough juice to
make a thin icing. Brush over the
biscuits while they are still warm.

Cook's Tip These biscuits are delicious
served with ice cream or creamy
desserts.

Date Crunch

Makes 24

INGREDIENTS

225g/8oz packet sweetmeal biscuits
75g/3oz/¹⁄₃ cup butter
30ml/2 tbsp golden syrup
75g/3oz/¹⁄₂ cup stoned dates, finely chopped
75g/3oz sultanas
150g/5oz milk or plain chocolate, chopped

Cook's Tip For an alternative topping, drizzle 75g/3oz melted white and 75g/3oz melted dark chocolate over.

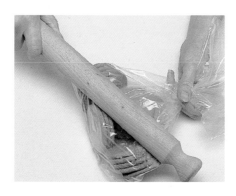

1 Line an 18cm/7in square shallow cake tin with foil. Put the biscuits in a plastic bag and crush roughly with a rolling pin.

2 Gently heat the butter and syrup in a small saucepan until the butter has melted.

3 Stir in the crushed biscuits, the dates and sultanas and mix well. Spoon into the prepared tin, press flat with the back of a spoon and chill for 1 hour.

4 Melt the chocolate in a heatproof bowl, over a saucepan of hot water, stirring until smooth. Spoon over the cookie mixture, spreading evenly with a palette knife. Chill until set. Lift the foil out of the cake tin and peel away. Cut the crunch into 24 pieces and arrange on a plate.

Peanut Cookies

Packing up a picnic? Got a birthday party coming up?
Make sure some of these nutty cookies are on the menu.

Makes 25

❦

INGREDIENTS

225g/8oz/1 cup butter
30ml/2 tbsp smooth peanut butter
115g/4oz/1 cup icing sugar
50g/2oz/½ cup cornflour
225g/8oz/2 cups plain flour
115g/4oz/1 cup unsalted peanuts

❦

1 Put the butter and peanut butter in a bowl and beat together. Add the icing sugar, cornflour and plain flour and mix together to make a soft dough.

2 Preheat the oven to 180°C/350°F/ Gas 4. Lightly oil two baking sheets. Roll the mixture into 25 small balls, using your hands and place on the baking sheets. Leave plenty of room for the cookies to spread.

3 Press the tops of the balls of dough flat, using either the back of a fork or your fingertips.

4 Press a few of the peanuts into each of the cookies. Bake for 15–20 minutes, until lightly browned. Leave to cool for a few minutes before lifting them carefully on to a wire rack with a palette knife.

Cook's Tip Make really monster cookies by rolling bigger balls of dough. Remember to leave plenty of room on the baking sheets for them to spread, though.

Apricot Yogurt Cookies

These soft cookies are very quick to make and are useful for lunch boxes.

Makes 16

INGREDIENTS

175g/6oz/1½ cups plain flour
5ml/1 tsp baking powder
5ml/1 tsp ground cinnamon
75g/3oz/1 cup rolled oats
75g/3oz/½ cup light muscovado sugar
115g/4oz/¾ cup chopped ready-to-eat dried apricots
15ml/1 tbsp flaked hazelnuts or almonds
150g/5oz/⅔ cup natural yogurt
45ml/3 tbsp sunflower oil
demerara sugar, for sprinkling

1 Preheat the oven to 190°C/375°F/ Gas 5. Lightly oil a large baking sheet.

2 Sift together the flour, baking powder and cinnamon. Stir in the oats, sugar, apricots and nuts.

Cook's Tip These cookies do not keep well, so it is best to eat them within two days, or to freeze them. Pack into polythene bags and freeze for up to four months.

3 Beat together the yogurt and oil, then stir evenly into the flour mixture to make a firm dough. If necessary, add a little more yogurt. Use your hands to roll the mixture into about 16 small balls.

4 Place the balls on the prepared baking sheet and flatten with a fork. Sprinkle with demerara sugar. Bake for 15–20 minutes, until firm and golden brown. Transfer to a wire rack and leave to cool.